£7.99

CONTEMPORARY GERMAN WRITERS

D0744032

HERTA MÜLLER

RENEWALS 458-4574
DATE DUE

Series Editor

Rhys W. Williams has been Professor of German and Head of the German Department at University of Wales, Swansea, since 1984. He has published extensively on the literature of German Expressionism and on the post-war novel. He is Director of the Centre for Contemporary German Literature at University of Wales, Swansea.

CONTEMPORARY GERMAN WRITERS

Series Editor: Rhys W. Williams

HERTA MÜLLER

edited by

Brigid Haines

CARDIFF
UNIVERSITY OF WALES PRESS
1998

British Library Cataloguing-in-Publication Data.
A catalogue record for this book is available from the British Library.

ISBN 0–7083–1484–8

Cover design by Olwen Fowler, The Beacon Studio, Roch.
Printed in Great Britain by Gwasg Dinefwr, Llandybïe.

Contents

List of Contributors

Owen Evans is Lecturer in German at the University of Wales Bangor. The author of a book and recent articles on Günter de Bruyn, he is currently compiling the section 'German Literature from 1945 to the Present Day' for the *YWMLS*.

Brigid Haines is Lecturer in German at the University of Wales Swansea. The author of a book on Adalbert Stifter (1991), she has also published articles on Andreas-Salomé, Aichinger, Königsdorf, Wolf, Jelinek and Moníková.

Dagmar von Hoff is *Wissenschaftliche Assistentin* at the University of Hamburg and Director of the Arbeitsstelle für feministische Literaturwissenschaft. The author of *Dramen des Weiblichen. Deutsche Dramatikerinnen um 1800* (1989), she has also published on Lenz, Günderrode, Warburg, Duras, Bernhard and Jelinek, as well as numerous articles on film and theatre.

Margaret Littler is Senior Lecturer in German at the University of Manchester. The author of a book on Alfred Andersch (1991), she has also published widely on post-war German women writers. She is a co-editor of *German Life and Letters*, and editor of the volume *Gendering German Studies* (1997).

David Midgley is University Lecturer in German and Fellow of St John's College, Cambridge. He has published widely on twentieth-century German authors, and is currently completing a book on the literature of the Weimar Republic.

Ricarda Schmidt is Senior Research Fellow in German at the University of Manchester. She has published widely on contemporary women's writing, GDR literature and literary theory. She is currently working on E.T.A. Hoffmann.

John J. White is Professor of German and Comparative Literature at King's College London. He is the author of *Mythology in the Modern Novel* (1971) and *Literary Futurism* (1990), and has co-edited volumes on Broch, Grass, Kafka, Mann, Musil, Stramm, Berlin in literature, and the Gruppe 47. He is currently writing a second monograph on Brecht and a critical survey of the German fiction of *Lebensraum*.

Preface

Contemporary German Writers

Each volume of the Contemporary German Writers series is devoted to an author who has spent a period as Visiting Writer at the Centre for Contemporary German Literature in the Department of German at the University of Wales, Swansea. The first chapter in each volume contains an original, previously unpublished piece by the writer concerned; the second consists of a biographical sketch, outlining the main events of the author's life and setting the works in context, particularly for the non-specialist or general reader. A third chapter will, in each case, contain an interview with the author, normally conducted during the writer's stay in Swansea. Subsequent chapters will contain contributions by invited British and German academics and critics on aspects of the writer's *œuvre*. While each volume will seek to provide both an overview of the author and some detailed analysis of individual works, the nature of that critical engagement will inevitably depend on the relative importance of the author concerned and on the amount of critical material which his or her work has previously inspired. Each volume includes an extensive bibliography designed to fill any gaps or remedy deficiencies in existing bibliographies. The intention is to produce in each case a book which will serve both as an introduction to the writer concerned and as a resource for specialists in contemporary German literature.

Herta Müller

The present volume opens with a contribution by Herta Müller herself, consisting of ten short texts originally written to accompany collages. After the brief outline biography, the interview with the author ranges over Müller's classification of her works as 'autofictions', her relationship to the German and Romanian languages, her poetics of 'die erfundene Wahrnehmung', her attitude to feminism, the significance of city life in *Reisende auf einem Bein*, the theme of friendship in *Herztier*, and the discrediting of the concept of utopia in the Eastern bloc states. The remaining chapters are intended to provide critical analysis of selected texts that have not been dealt with thoroughly elsewhere, and to treat certain key themes which run thoughout Müller's œuvre. David Midgley provides a close reading of *Der Mensch ist ein großer Fasan auf der Welt*, exploring the ways in which emotional experience is invested in objects which then take on increased significance in the text; this technique is typical of Müller's work as a whole. Margaret Littler compares the treatment of city life in Müller's *Reisende auf einem Bein* and two novels by the Czech writer Libuše Moníková, and argues that the modern city offers multiple possibilities for the postmodern female subject to explore new, shifting identities. Ricarda Schmidt explores the use of metaphor and metonymy in the densely structured novel *Herztier* and relates this to Müller's concept of morality; she exposes a tension between Müller's desire to denounce uniformity and her own imposition of uniformity through aesthetic patterning. John J. White reads Müller's texts against their historical background, arguing that they are 'palimpsests of the political', reflecting indirectly twentieth-century Romania's various experiences of totalitarian rule. Dagmar von Hoff argues that Müller asserts the place of morality within literature and exploits its expression through the poetic moment as a way of offering resistance to dictatorship. Brigid Haines takes up the theme of resistance and argues that Müller's entire œuvre, her essays as well as the literary works, including the latest novel *Heute wär ich mir lieber nicht begegnet*, may fruitfully be read in terms of her 'micro-politics of resistance'. Finally Owen Evans's extensive bibliography brings up to date the bibliography compiled by Dagmar Eke and published in 1991, and thus provides an invaluable resource for future researchers. The Centre for Contemporary German Literature is particularly pleased that this volume coincides with the award to Herta Müller of the International IMPAC Dublin Literary Award.

Abbreviations

Full bibliographical details appear in Chapter 10.

N	*Niederungen* (1982)
DT	*Drückender Tango* (1984)
MFW	*Der Mensch ist ein großer Fasan auf der Welt* (1986)
BF	*Barfüßiger Februar* (1987)
RB	*Reisende auf einem Bein* (1989)
TS	*Der Teufel sitzt im Spiegel. Wie Wahrnehmung sich erfindet* (1991)
FJ	*Der Fuchs war damals schon der Jäger* (1992)
KB	*Eine warme Kartoffel ist ein warmes Bett* (1992)
WK	*Der Wächter nimmt seinen Kamm* (1993)
HT	*Herztier* (1994)
HS	*Hunger und Seide* (1995)
FA	*In der Falle* (1996)
HB	*Heute wär ich mir lieber nicht begegnet* (1997)

1

Im Haarknoten wohnt eine Dame.
Zehn Texte

HERTA MÜLLER

ich sah die Tische im Spiegel

zwei Augen verglast

von weitem ganz nah

ein Pickel blühte an der Bar

vielleicht auf der Haut

vielleicht auf dem Glas

so gelb wie Schellenkraut

weil ich seit 14 Jahren hier saß

brachte der Kellner

den frischen Schnitt

seiner Wunde am Daumen mit

Sterne am Weg wie Kamillen

Augen lecken Tinte im Schlaf

morgen wenn sie sich öffnen

schreit in der Achsel ein Hahn

um den Tisch sitzen Ausgehhosen

Fahnen rot geschminkt

ein Herr kostet das Wasser

und ich sage

es geschah in aller Stille

er schaute als wäre ich

ein schwarzes Kraut im Licht

ich schwöre dir sagt er

dein Hirn paßt sowieso

in diesen Teller

die Nacht trug diese Gegend am Finger

Kisten mit unseren Namen

ruinierte nervöse Adressen

und Autos wie glühende Zimmer

sie fuhren und meinten es anders

ich aß einen Apfel wie immer

unerwartet ging ihm das Fleisch aus

es ist wahr daß ich zu lachen begann

wie die Schlüssel der Frau von nebenan

Die Pflanzen verstecken den Kopf

wie wir alle Mütze und Schal

die wachsen im Schlafen

Da platzen die Schalen

haben es eilig zurück in die Erde

an der Leine darunter verrutscht dann

ein Knochen

In dieser Nacht starb ein Mann auf der Straße

tags zuvor ging das Gerücht um

und ich glaub es schon wieder

daß Möwen auf dem Pflaster sitzen

schwarz wie Advokaten

im Federhaus wohnt ein Hahn

im Laubhaus die Allee

ein Hase wohnt im Fellhaus

im Wasserhaus ein See

im Eckhaus – die Patrouille

stößt einen vom Balkon dort

über dem Holunder

dann war es wieder Selbstmord

im Papierhaus wohnt die Stellungnahme

im Haarknoten wohnt eine Dame

kurz darauf sagt Barbara

mein Vater war Nazi

mein Sohn ist ein Skin

mein Mann Demokrazi

mit Doppelkinn

meine Tochter die wird Sängerin

Türflügel zur Altstadt

wo jeder seinen Vogel hat

die Goldkette mit Kreuz am Hals

hängt Jesus wie ein Wickelkind

der Taxifahrer sagt Sie sind

sicher nicht von hier

seltsam so was spüren wir

er ist ein betagter Mann

Käfig mit Beichtstuhl Anwalt Hausarzt

Apparat aus deutschem Zwirn und Galle

an seinem Hals kommt Jesus

ins Wanken wie eine Mausefalle

Wechselstuben in den Brüsten

Äpfel Birnen Fallobst dran

wenn wir uns jetzt lieben müßten

finge ich zu rascheln an

die Pflaumenbäume stutzt im Himmel der Friseur

auf der Leiter die einmal sein Armband war

oder sogar die Schnur vom Schuh

ein Kompagnon ein Schlaumeier oder Flaneur

– und alle anderen die starben sehen zu

ab und an steht einer auf

geht durch den Tabak seine Haare holen

und kommt zurück und pfeift

denn im Tabak blühen hellrosa Pistolen

und setzt sich hin und wird sekundenkahl

vom General mit Ameisen geschoren

häufig laufe ich ins Leben

und komm in einen Schuhkarton

ein Zentrum wird es darin geben

in Erfurt auch und Iserlohn

ein Rentner und ein Pendler in der Ecke

ein Nachtschichtler mit hellen Zehen

und die letzten fünf Zemtsäcke

die schwer zu fassen in Hannover stehen

2

Herta Müller:
Outline Biography

BRIGID HAINES

1953	Born in Nitzkydorf, a Swabian village in the Romanian Banat. Father a former member of the SS.
1968	Moved to Timişoara to attend the 'Gymnasium'.
1972	Became a member of the *Aktionsgruppe Banat*; other members included Richard Wagner and Rolf Bossert.
1972–6	Studied 'Germanistik' and 'Romänistik' at the University of Timişoara.
1975	*Aktionsgruppe Banat* suppressed by the Romanian authorities.
1976–9	Worked as a translator in a factory until sacked for refusal to collaborate with the secret police (*Securitate*).
1979–83	Worked sporadically as a German teacher.
1982	*Niederungen*, a collection of prose pieces about village life in the Banat, published in Romania to accusations from fellow Swabians of 'Nestbeschmutzung'.
1984	*Niederungen* published in the Federal Republic to critical acclaim; the prose pieces *Drückender Tango* published in Romania.
1986	Publication of *Der Mensch ist ein großer Fasan auf der Welt*, a novel about ethnic Germans leaving Romania. Death by suicide of Rolf Bossert in the Federal Republic.
1987	Müller left for West Berlin with her then husband, Richard Wagner; publication of *Barfüßiger Februar*, a collection of prose pieces about life in Romania; awarded the *Ricarda-Huch-Preis der Stadt Darmstadt*.
1989	Publication of the Berlin novel *Reisende auf einem Bein*; awarded the *Marieluise-Fleißer-Preis der Stadt Ingolstadt*. Death of friend Roland Kirsch. Fall of the Ceauşescu

regime in Romania; death of Nicolae and Elena Ceauşescu.

1989–90 Writer in Residence at the University of Paderborn during the winter semester; this resulted in the first volume of essays on Müller's work: Norbert Otto Eke (ed.), *Die erfundene Wahrnehmung* (1991).

1990 Awarded the *Roswitha-Gedankenmedaille der Stadt Bad Gandersheim*.

1991 Publication of *Der Teufel sitzt im Spiegel. Wie Wahrnehmung sich erfindet*, a volume of poetological essays; awarded the *Kranichsteiner Literaturpreis*, and a writer's grant from the Villa-Massimo in Rome.

1992 Publication of the novel *Der Fuchs war damals schon der Jäger* and of *Eine warme Kartoffel ist ein warmes Bett*, a volume of essays written for the Swiss magazine *Du*; awarded the *Kritikerpreis des Verbandes deutscher Schriftsteller*.

1994 Publication of the novel *Herztier*, based on the experiences of the members of the *Aktionsgruppe Banat*; awarded the *Kleist-Preis*.

1995 Publication of the volume of essays *Hunger und Seide*, and of the collages *Der Wächter nimmt seinen Kamm*; awarded the *Europäischer Literaturpreis Aristeion* and became a member of the *Deutsche Akademie für Sprache und Dichtung*.

1995–6 Writer in Residence at the Ruhr-Universität Bochum during the winter semester; this resulted in the second volume of essays on Müller's work: Ralph Köhnen (ed.), *Der Druck der Erfahrung treibt die Sprache in die Dichtung* (1997).

1996 Publication of the volume of literary essays, *In der Falle*. Writer in Residence at Dickinson College, Carlisle, USA during the spring semester; an interview with Müller and two papers arising out of her USA trip were published in *Monatshefte*, 89/4 (1997). Writer in Residence at the Centre for Contemporary German Literature in the Department of German, University of Wales Swansea during the autumn semester.

1997 Publication of the novel *Heute wär ich mir lieber nicht begegnet*; awarded the *Literaturpreis der Stadt Graz*.

1998   Awarded the *Ida-Dehmel-Literaturpreis*; also awarded the *International IMPAC Dublin Literary Award* for *The Land of Green Plums*, the English translation of *Herztier*.

3

Gespräch mit Herta Müller

BRIGID HAINES UND MARGARET LITTLER

BH: Deine Werke sind alle in gewissem Maße autobiographisch, aber die autobiographischen Elemente sind stark literarisch bearbeitet. In *Der Teufel sitzt im Spiegel* zitierst Du David Hare: »Die Person, die schreibt, bin nicht ich«. Wie würdest Du Dein Verhältnis mit Adine, Irene, dem Ich in *Niederungen* und *Herztier* usw. charakterisieren?

HM: Soweit ich mich in der Literatur orientiert habe, habe ich mir Autoren ausgesucht, bei denen das strikt Biographische in der Literatur drin ist. Es ist nicht zufällig, daß ich dadurch viele Bücher gelesen habe über Nationalsozialismus, geschrieben von den Opfern. Das waren natürlich die extremsten Beispiele: Konzentrationslager, oder Lager insgesamt, auch Arbeitslager, Gulag, zum Beispiel in der Sowjetunion. Es ist immer für mich diese Gruppe von Autoren, wie zum Beispiel Primo Levi, Jorge Semprun, Ruth Klüger, Alexander Solschenizyn, Imre Kertész oder Paul Celan, die in ihrer Biographie keine Wahl hatten. In der Person liegen die Dinge so schwer, daß das vorderste Bedürfnis das ist, mit dem, was passiert ist, zurechtzukommen. Die staatliche Macht zwang diesen Autoren ihr Thema auf, und mir ging es genauso: Das Thema wurde mir aufgezwungen, ich habe es mir nicht gesucht. Sowie mir das Leben aufgezwungen wurde. Es ist keine freie Entscheidung, und das eine bedingt das andere.

BH: Es ist aber keine Autobiographie, was Du schreibst.

HM: Nein, überhaupt nicht. Georges Arthur Goldschmidt sagt über seine Bücher »autofiktional«. Mir hat das Wort sehr eingeleuchtet, und das ist auch genau das, was Du gesagt hast, also natürlich eigene Erfahrung als Hintergrund, aber sehr stark literarisch bearbeitet, und dadurch wird das Fiktion. Also ich habe überhaupt nichts in meinen Büchern so aufgeschrieben, wie es war. Ich brauche aber diese sichere Beziehung zu der Erfahrung, um in die Fiktion zu gehen. Die fiktionale Realität muß auch bei der Rezeption ihre Glaubwürdigkeit haben. Dafür ist diese Erfahrung wichtig. Ich muß vielleicht zwanzig Verhöre erlebt haben, damit ich eines erfinde.

BH: Das nächste Thema wäre Deine zwei Sprachen: Du sprichst also Deutsch als Muttersprache und Rumänisch als zweite Sprache, oder könnte man sagen, als zweite Muttersprache? In *Hunger und Seide* hast Du sie als »zwei genormte Möglichkeiten, die Welt anzusehen« beschrieben. Kannst Du das etwas weiter erklären?
HM: Der Unterschied bleibt schon, daß das Deutsche die Muttersprache ist, weil ich Rumänisch viel zu spät gelernt habe. Als ich anfing, Rumänisch wirklich zu sprechen und als der Alltag in dieser Sprache verlief, war ich schon fünfzehn und in der Stadt. Früher hatte ich Rumänisch nur drei Stunden pro Woche als Fremdsprache in der deutschen Schule gelernt. Es ist was anderes als eine zweite Muttersprache, aber auch was anderes als eine Fremdsprache, weil man in ihr lebt. Es ist eine Intimität entstanden, die schon mit der Muttersprache zu tun hat, die ähnlich ist wie bei der Muttersprache, aber trotzdem hätte ich zum Beispiel nie auf Rumänisch schreiben gekonnt, und es ist mir nie in den Sinn gekommen, es zu versuchen.
BH: Aber die Sprache ist immer noch im Kopf dabei, wenn Du schreibst, weil Du manchmal Bilder aus dem Rumänischen benutzt.
HM: Ja, das ist aber was anderes. In zweisprachigen Gegenden ist das so, daß beide Sprachen sich in den Kopf hineinstellen und ihre Selbstverständlichkeit für sich bekommen, aber sich auch immer in Frage stellen, die eine die andere. Es läuft immer parallel. Und als Schriftstellerin profitiert man unglaublich davon; das ist das beste, was einem passieren kann. Wenn die Sprachen ähnlich wären, wie zum Beispiel Deutsch und Englisch es sind, wäre es nicht so unterschiedlich wie eine romanisch-slavische Sprache und Deutsch. Dieses Romänisch ist in seiner Sinnlichkeit und in seiner Art, auf die Welt zu blicken, völlig anders, und mir war diese Art, die Welt anzuschauen, immer näher. Die Sprachbilder, die Metaphorik, die Redewendungen, die Folklore haben immer viel mehr strukturell zu mir gepaßt als das, was in meiner eigenen Sprache vorhanden ist. Ich habe durch dieses späte Erlernen der

Sprache die nötige Distanz dazu gehabt. Wenn das Selbstverständnis allein in der Sprache da ist, entsteht diese Distanz nicht, und es wird einem gar nicht bewußt, wie schön ein Bild oder eine Redewendung ist. Ich habe natürlich damit viel gearbeitet, weil es mich fasziniert hat. Ich habe das Beispiel mit dem Fasan schon öfter gegeben: Der deutsche Fasan ist der Prahler, der selbstsichere, arrogante Mensch; der rumänische Fasan ist der Verlierer, der seinem Leben nicht gewachsen ist, der Vogel, der nicht fliegen kann, und der, weil er nicht fliegen kann und ziemlich groß und schwer ist, von der Kugel des Jägers getroffen wird. Die eine Sprache nimmt sich nur das Aussehen, das Federkleid des Vogels, und stuft ihn ein, und die andere Sprache nimmt seine Existenz und stuft sie ein, und sieht ihn in der Gefahr. Mich hat dieses Bild mit dem Verlierer überzeugt und nicht das, was ich in meiner eigenen Sprache habe. Insofern hat diese Sprache mir ständig Sachen gezeigt, wie sie anders sein können, als ich sie in meiner eigenen Sprache habe.

BH: In *Der Teufel sitzt im Spiegel* sprichst Du von der »erfundenen Wahrnehmung«, die ich einerseits als eine Art zu schreiben verstehe, womit man genaue Beobachtungen mit Phantasie und Traum verbindet, aber andererseits auch eine Methode zu sein scheint, politisch oppositionell zu sein. Die erfundene Wahrnehmung ist also sowohl eine ästhetische als auch eine politische Haltung. Habe ich das richtig verstanden?
HM: Es wird immer wieder darüber diskutiert, was ist politisch? Je mehr Restriktionen es in einem Staat gibt, wird ja das vordergründig politisch, wodurch ein System sich angegriffen fühlt. Insofern ist das Politische sehr oft da, weil das System sich attackiert fühlt, weil es meint, daß es Dimensionen gibt, und das sind sehr wohl auch die ästhetischen Dimensionen, die unberechenbar sind. Dadurch wird das Ästhetische als Phänomen ein vordergründiger politischer Faktor in einer Diktatur, weil das Regime das so sieht. Das kommt in erster Linie als Reaktion des Staates und nicht von einem selbst. Die Ästhetik hat natürlich jede Diktatur beschäftigt und die Zensur ist der sichtbarste Ausdruck dafür. Jede Ästhetik hat natürlich ihre politische Haltung, ob man das will oder nicht, weil ein System sehr wohl unterscheidet, welche Kunst es akzeptiert, und warum.
BH: Hat sich Deine Ästhetik verändert, seitdem Du im Westen lebst, weil der Druck nicht mehr da ist?

HM: Ich weiß es nicht, ich kann das nicht beurteilen. Es ist nicht etwas, was man bewußt macht. Das Thema verlangt seine Sprache. Der Ortswechsel war nicht so wichtig wie die zeitliche Distanz: Mit zwanzig war ich im Kopf völlig anders, als ich es mit Mitte vierzig bin. Das Biologische des Körpers ist im Schreiben auch genauso drin, wie es in allen anderen Dingen drin ist. Man hat ja so viel Leben dazu gekriegt, und anderes ist weiter weggerückt. Man denkt ja über sich immer wieder nach; es bleibt einem nichts erspart. Man sieht sich selber ganz anders zwanzig Jahre später: Man kann sich nicht mehr bruchlos identifizieren mit der Person, die man war.

ML: Die Redewendung »der Teufel sitzt im Spiegel« scheint mehrere Bedeutungen zu haben: Sie hat einerseits mit Selbsterkenntnis zu tun, mit zwanghafter Gruppenidentität, auch mit der Verletzlichkeit der Mächtigen, und ich wollte fragen, ob Du den Begriff etwas näher erklären könntest?
HM: Du hast ja fast alle Sachen gesagt! Ich bin davon ausgegangen, wie unter so einem auf den ersten Blick harmlosen Spruch, den ich aus einem bäuerlichen Milieu von zu Hause kenne, all diese Verbote sind, und wie früh das einsetzt. Die Familie paßt genau auf, daß sie einen in der Hand behält, wie es ein Staat auch tut, aus ganz anderen Gründen natürlich und mit unvergleichbaren Methoden. Es ist trotzdem in der Familie angesiedelt, und es besteht diese Angst, daß das Individuelle sich behauptet, und das Individuelle wird immer von vornherein als ein potentieller Gegner des ganzen Institutionellen angesehen. Man meint, diese Art von harmlosem Spruch bezieht sich nur auf schöne Kleider oder irgendetwas ganz Äußerliches, aber man sieht, wie er sehr wohl und sehr gezielt in ganz andere Dinge hineingeht. Das ist eine Form von Indoktrinierung. Man setzt den Leuten etwas in den Kopf durch eine harmlose Floskel, was dann später aber fest sitzt und was dann in allen möglichen anderen Lebenssituationen wieder wirkt. Dadurch hat man Menschen im Griff. Die erste Diktatur, die ich kannte, war das banatschwäbische Dorf. Ich habe eine blasse Variante der Überschaubarkeit und des Genormtwerdens erlebt, danach das richtig Zuschlagende, und ich war mit gewissen Grundlinien vertraut.

BH: In *Der Teufel sitzt im Spiegel* schreibst Du, daß Du gegen das kontinuierliche oder chronologische Erzählen bist. Siehst Du diese Arten von Erzählen als zu autoritär?
HM: Kontinuierliches, chronologisches Erzählen muß nicht per se autoritär sein. Ich schreibe in dieser Diskontinuität, die im Grunde genommen auch ihre Kontinuitäten hat. Es sind immer mehrere Ebenen, aber sie werden dann auch natürlich in ihrer Lage fortgesetzt. Ganz ohne Kontinuität kommt man nicht aus, sonst bindet sich nichts zusammen. Es muß ja alles irgendwo hinwollen und muß ja auch irgendwohin gelangen. Ich kann aber so wenig einlinige, einspurige oder eingleisige zeitliche Folge erkennen, ich kann sie auch so wenig in der Welt erkennen. Es passieren immer so viele Dinge auf einmal. Um die Dinge handhabbar zu machen und sie auf uns zu beziehen, vereinfachen wir sie und fügen sie zu in sich geschlossene Vorgänge zusammen, aber im Grunde genommen sind sie alle zerstreut. Ich glaube auch, daß äußere Dinge, Gegenstände in das Tun von Menschen auch mit hineinwirken. Durch diese unterbrochene Art zu erzählen habe ich mehr Möglichkeiten, als wenn ich an einem Faden entlang erzählen würde. Ich bin ja auch von diesem Sozialistischen Realismus ein gebranntes Kind. Darum ist für mich wahrscheinlich auch das Bedürfnis nach Fiktionalem so groß, und nach Literarisiertem und nach dem Raum, der diese Realität über sich hinauswirbelt, wo die Dinge dann auch schweben und wo ästhetisch oder poetisch die Spannung entsteht. Träume spielen in meinen Texten eine große Rolle, und ich weiß auch nicht, wo das Surreale anfängt. Für mich ist Surrealität nicht etwas anderes als Realität, sondern eine tiefere Realität.
BH: Wird der Leser zum Mitgestalter des Textes?
HM: Ich mache mir über den Leser gar keine Gedanken! Man ist in Deutschland so oft versucht, Metaphorik zu sehen, wo es für mich nackte Realien sind. In *Fuchs* habe ich so oft gehört: »Die Pappeln sind Messer«. Ich sage: »Nein!«. Ich setze schon manchmal eine Metapher, aber ich löse sie später durch eine Realität auf, wie in dem *Herztier* zum Beispiel mit der Nuß: Da hat die Freundin einen Krebsknoten unterm Arm und der hat die Größe einer Nuß. Insofern habe ich diese Metapher gezwungen, strikte Realität zu werden. Ich befinde mich auch immer vor dem Problem, wie beschreibt man Diktatur? Es wäre ja furchtbar, ein pädagogisches, ideologisches Buch zu schreiben mit umgekehrten Vorzeichen, wie

es im Sozialismus selber geschrieben werden sollte. Man kann kein holzig realistisches Buch über eine Diktatur schreiben.

ML: Ich möchte ein ganz anderes Thema anschlagen: In *Der Mensch ist ein großer Fasan auf der Welt* kommt der Tauschwert der Frauen in dieser Gesellschaft sehr deutlich zum Ausdruck. Ist dies ein bewußt feministischer Roman?

HM: Nein. Ich bin keine Feministin. Ich bin vielleicht eine Individualistin, und ich bin eine Frau. Ich versuche meine persönlichen Sachen in den Situationen, in die ich komme, zu verteidigen und dafür zu stehen. Ich habe keine Theorien. Es ist nur eine Realität, daß in Diktaturen sowie in allen Bereichen des Alltags natürlich auch das Sexuelle mißbraucht wird. Erotik ist für Machthaber immer eine sehr attraktive Form, jemanden zu erpressen. Es gibt gar nichts Besseres. Wenn man mit einer Frau schläft, hat man sie total in der Hand. Der Versuch, Beziehungen anzuknüpfen, wurde genauso eingesetzt wie das andere Instrumentarium, das die Macht hatte, um jemanden zu erledigen. Es wird alles verzerrt: einerseits aus der eigenen Emotionalität der jeweiligen Person, sprich der Frau natürlich. Es entsteht aber auch die Gewißheit, daß man durch sexuelle Beziehungen allerhand erreichen kann. Das kennt man auch im Westen, aber es hat in Diktaturen eine drastischere Wirkung. Andererseits ist in Rumänien die Männer- und Frauenrolle eine zum Teil unveränderte geblieben, wie man sie in westlichen Gesellschaften vor Jahrzehnten gekannt hat. Damit sich solche Rollen verändern, muß in einer Gesellschaft insgesamt einiges passieren. Die Frauenrolle in Rumänien war eine, wie man sie hierzulande von den Großeltern kennt. Das ist der Grund, weshalb diese Beziehungen so beschrieben sind.

ML: Wobei die Frauen realistischer sind als die Männer: die Mutter zum Beispiel akzeptiert den Tauschwert der Tochter, was der Vater nicht wahrhaben will. Er kommt mir naiv vor, und das scheint oft der Fall zu sein.

HM: Ja, wenn man die Rolle von Frauen in den bäuerlichen Milieus von außen sieht, ist sie bei Gott nicht eine souveräne, aber in den Alltagsdingen ist die Frau sehr pragmatisch und selbstsicher. Sie kriegt ihre Individualität von einem ganz anderen Punkt her. Sie hat eine gewisse Lebenstüchtigkeit, im richtigen Moment das Richtige zu tun und zu sagen: »So ist das einfacher. Ändern kann

man es sowieso nicht«. Lebenstüchtigkeit ist sehr oft aus moralischen Gesichtspunkten fragwürdig.

ML: Ich möchte Dich über die Bedeutung der Stadt in *Reisende auf
einem Bein* und auch in anderen Werken fragen. In *Herztier* zum
Beispiel fällt der Satz:»In einer Diktatur kann es keine Städte geben«, was ich als positive Aussage über die Stadt sehe. In *Reisende
auf einem Bein* bewohnt Irene die Stadt sehr gern, wenn auch stets
als Ausländerin im Ausland. Irene kommt mir wie ein Entwurf zu
einem postmodernen Subjekt vor, insofern, daß sie immer in Bewegung ist, nicht vom bewußten Verstand gelenkt, sondern von
einer fast körperlichen Beziehung zur Stadt. Trifft das zu?
HM: Ja, Stadt ist für mich insofern positiv, weil sie Anonymität
garantieren sollte. Natürlich hat Anonymität beide Seiten: An der
Anonymität kann man auch zerbrechen. Irene, die aus einem anderen Land kommt, von dem man im Buch sehr wohl erfährt, daß
es eine Diktatur ist, wünscht sich nicht gesehen zu werden, nicht
bekannt zu sein, Ruhe vor einer Überwachung zu haben: Das ist
das Positive. Sie will sich der Stadt körperlich annähern und sie
sich aneignen. Sie benötigt das Vertrauen, das im Augenblick an
einem gewissen Ort entsteht, und sie sucht das immer wieder. Das
ist natürlich nicht möglich, weil sie fremd ist. Dieser Versuch
scheitert auch immer wieder und macht die Fremdheit erst richtig
spürbar und macht sie erst richtig zum Schmerz.
ML: Zum Schluß des Romans gibt es dieses Bild:»Es gibt Bewohner mit Handgepäck und Reisende in dünnen Schuhen«, und Irene unterscheidet nicht mehr so stark dazwischen. Kommt da eine
erste Anpassung oder ein richtiges Bewohnen der Stadt vor, oder
wohnt sie immer noch im Ausnahmezustand?
HM: Ich weiß es nicht. Es ist ja auch nicht nur mitgebrachte
Fremdheit, es ist auch die Fremdheit, die immer wieder an Ort
und Stelle entsteht. Die anderen Personen, diese Männerfiguren,
der Schwule oder der Franz, sind auch fremd. Sie gehören nicht
mehr zur Stadt, weil sie nachdenken, weil sie sich vergegenwärti-
gen, was, wann, wie passiert. Ich glaube nicht, daß es das Ideale
ist, nicht fremd zu sein. Die ideale Beziehung zu einer Umgebung
ist aus meiner Sicht eine Fremdheit, an die man sich gewöhnt.
Fremdheit kann nicht ausgetragen werden, weil sie eine Modalität
der Wahrnehmung ist. Bewußte Wahrnehmung und kritische Sicht
werden immer Fremdheit zur Folge haben.

ML: Das kommt sehr schön im Calvino-Zitat zum Ausdruck, wo Irene mit der Stadt identifiziert wird.

HM: . . . Du meinst, »wenn man sie von außen sieht, ist sie was anderes, als wenn man hineingeht«; ja, ja.

BH: Wie ist der Roman *Der Fuchs war damals schon der Jäger* entstanden? War das zuerst ein Filmprojekt?

HM: Ich war ziemlich oft neidisch auf den Film, auf die Möglichkeiten, mit Bildern und mit Text Hand in Hand etwas zu machen und auch auf die Arbeit im Kollektiv, weil man als Schriftsteller immer allein sitzt. Ich habe mit Harry Merkle ein Drehbuch geschrieben, und es wurde verfilmt, aber es ist leider aus verschiedenen Gründen kein guter Film geworden. Und dann habe ich gesagt, jetzt will ich daraus etwas anderes machen.

BH: Jetzt kommen wir zum *Herztier*. Wenn ich es richtig verstanden habe, geht es in diesem Roman darum, wie schwer es war, Freundschaften wachzuhalten, aber auch wie wichtig.

HM: Die Gruppe von Freunden in diesem Roman ist nicht nur für sich selber eine Gruppe, sondern für den Staat auch. Der Staat sieht auch das Wir. Dadurch werden Freundschaften überstrapaziert. Die Freunde wollen das Leben des anderen erträglich machen und das können sie, aber nur zum Teil, weil die äußere Realität immer wieder hineinsticht in dieses Leben. Die Freundschaft kann höchstens so viel garantieren, daß der Einzelne nicht allein zerbricht. Aber daß er nicht zerbricht, das kann sie nicht leisten. Das ist ja das, was so weh tut. Jede persönliche Nähe ist dem, was der Staat im Sinn hat und tut, nicht gewachsen. Die Freundschaft kann nicht retten. Und man wünscht sich das, man will das so gerne für sich von den anderen und man will das den anderen auch bieten können. Aber es geht nicht.

BH: Und kannst Du in diesem Kontext etwas über den Begriff »Herztier« sagen, was, wie ich es sehe, mit der eigenen Verletzlichkeit, mit der Intimität mit den anderen und mit der Diktatur zu tun hat?

HM: Ich kann das nicht erklären: Das ist genau das, was ich in diesem Buch nicht gemacht habe. In jeder Situation muß das Herztier für sich sprechen. Es muß für sich sprechen, wenn die Großmutter dem Kind zum ersten Mal sagt, »Ruh Dein Herztier aus, Du hast heute so viel gespielt«, wenn die Großmutter dem

Großvater sagt, »Dein Herztier ist eine Maus«, wenn dann die Ich-Person am Fluß den Freunden sagt, »Unsere Herztiere ziehen aus« bevor sie die Stadt verlassen, wenn die Ich-Person im Studenten-haus den Kühlschrank öffnet, und das Licht an der Lampe ist für sie das Herztier des Diktators: Es muß jedes Herztier in dem Kon-text, in dem es steht und in der Person, in der es verankert ist, für sich sprechen. Es ist nichts genau Bestimmbares. Es wird nicht klar, ob das Herztier rettet, oder ob es das ist, was an einem zer-stört oder verletzt wird. Das weiß ich auch nicht. Ich wollte dieses Wort ausbalancieren, daß es immer woandershin schillert.

BH: Ist es der Kern der Persönlichkeit?

HM: Vielleicht, ja.

ML: Und immer was anderes, nichts, was man verallgemeinern kann.

HM: Ja, und bei jedem was anderes.

ML: Eine kurze aber große Frage zum Thema Utopie –

HM: Ich kann's nicht mehr hören.

ML: Kannst Du einfach sagen, warum das ein überholter Begriff ist?

HM: Ja, weil ich nicht so genau weiß, wozu eine Utopie gut sein soll. Durch eine Utopie kann keine Gesellschaft verändert oder verbessert werden.

BH: Vielleicht ist es bloß das falsche Wort. Ich sehe das Problem darin, wie man überhaupt politisch engagiert sein kann, wenn man die Verhältnisse nicht verbessern will? Das ist, was ich unter Utopie verstehe.

HM: Ich glaube nicht, daß das mit einer Utopie funktioniert. Hoff-nung ist etwas anderes. Bei einer Utopie habe ich Angst, daß es nicht das einzelne Detail ist, sondern daß es eben dieses große Übergestülpte ist. Wer kann heute in einer so komplizierten, zer-splitterten, diversifizierten Gesellschaft so etwas leisten? Und wer sollte sich das anmaßen?

BH: Aber politische Ziele kann man doch haben?

HM: Ja, natürlich. Aber jeder in seinem Bereich. Diese in die Rea-lität umgesetzten Utopien sind immer ein Unglück geworden. Sie haben immer eine Diktatur ergeben. Für mich ist das völlig lo-gisch. Wenn eine Idee über alles Bescheid weiß, kann sie ja nichts anderes tun, als den Einzelnen nötigen und zwingen. Der neue Mensch, der im Sozialismus geschaffen werden sollte, war ein Monstrum. Das Ich war nicht ein Bestandteil des Wir, sondern immer der Feind des Wir. Individualismus war das schlimmste Wort.

BH: Gemeinsame Ziele sind aber für die Politik nötig.

HM: Ja, man braucht ein Engagement und ein Wissen über die Fakten, in die man eingreifen will, und man braucht ganz verschiedene Leute, aber das ist etwas ganz anderes als eine Utopie.

ML: Könntest Du das Buch *In der Falle* kurz beschreiben?

HM: Es ist nur ein Büchlein mit Vorlesungen, die ich vor ein paar Jahren in Bonn gehalten habe. Ich habe über Autoren gesprochen, die an Diktaturen zerbrochen sind: Theodor Kramer, Ruth Klüger und Inge Müller.

BH: Bis jetzt sind bei Dir die literarischen Texte ästhetisch und vom Inhalt her immer viel abstrakter als das essayistische Werk gewesen, worin das rumänische Alltagsleben sehr ausführlich, spontan und gefühlvoll geschildert wird. Obwohl die Themen des jüngsten Romans *Heute wär ich mir lieber nicht begegnet* aber Kontinuitäten mit *Herztier* aufzeigen, erinnert der Roman auch sehr stark an *Hunger und Seide* und könnte vielleicht als dein persönlichstes Buch beschrieben werden. War das eine bewußte Änderung?

HM: Nein. Das Thema Diktatur zieht immer seine Kreise. In den Essays spreche ich darüber direkter, es sind sachliche Texte, oft auch notgedrungen polemisch. In den Romanen sucht sich das Thema ganz anders seinen Weg. Es muß literarischen Personen gehorchen. Diese machen, was geschieht, unter sich aus. So wendet sich nichts nach außen.

BH: Die rumänische Diktatur ist jetzt seit langem vorbei, aber die Aufgabe, die Effekte der Diktatur auf die Menschen zu beschreiben, kommt Dir anscheinend als wichtiger denn je vor. Kannst Du eine Zeit voraussehen, wo Du mit diesem Thema fertig werden wirst? Können wir zum Beispiel vielleicht eines Tages wieder so eine scharfe Analyse der bundesrepublikanischen Gesellschaft erwarten, wie Du sie einst in *Reisende auf einem Bein* geliefert hast?

HM: Ich muß das schreiben, was mich am meisten beschäftigt. Literatur ist doch immer von dort ausgegangen, wo beim Autor die Beschädigung am tiefsten war: Ich bin keine Ausnahme. Ich suche mir mein Thema nicht aus, ich werde von ihm abgeholt, sonst müßte ich doch nicht schreiben.

4

Remembered Things:
The Representation of Memory and Separation in
Der Mensch ist ein großer Fasan auf der Welt

DAVID MIDGLEY

Manchmal glaube ich, jeder trägt im Kopf einen Zeigefinger. Der zeigt auf das, was gewesen ist.
Herta Müller (*TS*, 9)

Herta Müller's early writings are characterized by an extraordinary vividness. The prose pieces in *Niederungen* (1984) are not uniformly bleak, but their most striking passages are those which give precise formulation to moments of intense and disturbing experience. Whether she is evoking childhood perceptions of adult behaviour or recording the debilitating impact on adult bodies of child-rearing and life's general depredations, whether she is expressing childhood fantasies generated by anxiety and the sense of isolation or reconstructing atrocities for which the parents' generation were responsible at war, Müller has a way of focusing attention on the specific image, the specific object, in which the significance of a remembered experience is concentrated.[1] In the story *Der Mensch ist ein großer Fasan auf der Welt* (1986), such moments of immediate sensory or emotional experience acquire additional resonance within the text. As references to particular objects recur, they carry forward the emotional significance vested in them by the experience of particular characters; and as more and more is revealed about the relationships between characters and about their past experiences, so the references to objects become vested with the poignancy of the memories and associations which constitute the very identity of the characters concerned.

The group of characters in question are German-speaking inhabitants of a Romanian village. They are connected both by the memories they share of their own lives and of each other's lives, and by their common interest in leaving the country. The tanner already has his passport and has sold up; at a later stage he writes from Stuttgart to those who are left behind. The carpenter and his wife have already sold their carpets, but are still waiting for their passports; it is in connection with their case that we learn that the local militia commonly expects sexual favours to be supplied in exchange for a passport (*MFW*, 51). The night-watchman opts to stay; at the end of the text we learn that he has found a.new wife. The figure whose personal fate we watch most closely, together with that of his family, is the miller, Windisch. While proper names are supplied for some of the other characters (forenames for the young, and surnames for the very old), Windisch is the only one of the group who is identified by his surname, whereas the others are identified by their trade or social function. Even Windisch's wife is mostly referred to only as Windisch's wife. The effect of this distinctive treatment is to give a special prominence to the personal experiences and the perspective of Windisch himself. On the very first page it is Windisch's memories and expectations that are foregrounded. He is approaching the war memorial on his way to the mill. He is counting the days and counting the years, as he does every morning. He counts the days until 'the end', i.e. until he and his family can leave; and he counts two years which, amongst other things, is the time that has elapsed since his wife has been refusing him sex after having a hysterectomy (*MFW*, 16).

Already on this first page of the text, the associated pain of emotional detachment and emotional adhesion is being signalled through the description of objects that have become familiar in Windisch's life. The opening section carries the title 'Die tiefe Stelle', which refers to a depression in the road. Windisch's bicycle shudders every morning when he rides over that depression, and every time he rides over it he is reminded that 'the end' is near. Nothing in the text suggests that the depression in the road is perceived as an indication of the rottenness of the regime (although there is clear evidence of that elsewhere), nor is there anything to suggest that it should be read as a symbol of Windisch's state of mind. The depression is simply there as a familiar feature of the landscape with which Windisch's life has for long been associated, a daily reminder of his situation and his expectations. Other familiar objects will come to represent the experiences of attachment and detachment in the course of the story. Household objects in particular acquire that resonance as they are gathered together ready for sale: cutlery is laid out on the window-sill, plates are set out on the floor, white patches are left on the walls where the cupboard had stood and the clock had hung (*MFW*, 19). Objects which are kept become emblems of the separation that is slowly taking place. Windisch's daughter Amalie has a glass tear-drop, a gift from the tanner's son Rudi. When filled with rainwater the glass yields a salt which makes the water taste like tears. The token of affection is also an emblem of grief. It is 'a glass tear-drop' that is said to stand on Windisch's cheek on the final page, when he and his wife have returned from Germany to visit the village (*MFW*, 111). At their moment of departure the heavens are said to be full of 'grey mountains of homesickness', and the depression in the road has become grey and craggy, as if it has grown old along with them (*MFW*, 105).

The phrase which gives the work its title, too, belongs among the motifs which acquire cumulative resonance as the story progresses. As a proverbial saying, it is part of the common linguistic currency of the land, a readily available expression of something about the human condition. Human beings stand upon this earth like big pheasants, it says. As it first occurs, spoken by the night-watchman (*MFW*, 8), the image is suggestive of strength, pride, self-sufficiency, self-importance, vanity; but in other contexts it can also appear to suggest clumsiness, haplessness, displacement, and by implication the yearning for the end of displacement, for a truer homeland, which is evidently what motivates Windisch's departure. As a ready-made phrase it presents itself to Windisch like a commentary from without on his own situation (by implication) and on that of his daughter (more explicitly). Windisch utters it, but with a voice that is 'not his' (*MFW*, 84), at a moment when he has observed Amalie's sexual self-esteem revealing itself. What Windisch observes again carries an echo of the ready-made wisdom of the night-watchman, who expects a young woman's transition to sexual experience to express itself in her bearing, in the way she sets her feet upon the ground. That is what Windisch observes in Amalie, that is what apparently prompts the comment in a voice that is not his own. But there is more to this recurrence of the proverbial saying than merely a confirmation of the token of masculine stereotyping which has passed between Windisch and the night-watchman. It is made explicit in the text that Amalie is no sexual innocent (*MFW*, 66 f.); but enough has also been revealed about the context of Windisch's situation for it to be apparent that the principal reason for her self-conscious presentation of her sexuality is that it has fallen to her to pay the price for the family's exit permit. It is she who has to make the visits to the militiaman for the passports, and to the priest for the baptism certificates. The expression of her sexual self-confidence is also an intimation of her sexual subjugation; and as such it is a reminder of Windisch's own helplessness in the situation. In the circumstances of Ceauşescu's Romania, Amalie is aware that her body is a more valuable commodity than the products of her father's labours, and she does not blush to tell him so, echoing the contemptuous words of others: 'Mit deinem Mehl kommst du nicht weit' (*MFW*, 88). Amalie's self-regard and Windisch's haplessness are two complementary dimensions of the human predicament evoked in this work. The term 'Mensch' being gender-neutral, both of these dimensions can be seen to be suggested by the phrase 'Der Mensch ist ein großer Fasan auf der Welt'.[2]

The moments of Amalie's sexual submission to figures in authority are not directly narrated. What we are shown is how she recalls them, as a conflation of physical sensations and observations: the militiaman's mouth on her neck, the weight of the priest's thighs, impressions of the silver cross that hangs from the militiaman's neck, a glimpse of the altar through an open door (*MFW*, 102 f.). What is remarkable about this representation of what she has to undergo is not just the avoidance of any manifest expression of outrage, but the way in which her experiences are set in an ironic relationship to a network of other human experiences recalled in the text. Amalie's recollections are framed by two statements which exemplify the way the older generation resort to cliché in their responses to adversity. The first of these statements is a remark made by the tailor when he comes to buy the family's carpets. In that context, Windisch's wife is probably thinking of the experience of selling up when she speaks of not being able to escape fate; when the tailor replies, 'Ich weiß nicht [. . .] Er hat nichts Böses auf der Welt getan' (*MFW*, 100), then he is probably thinking of his son Dietmar, with whom Amalie has had a sexual liaison, and who has subsequently died in a shooting accident. It is the recollection of that statement which is said to give Amalie a burning sensation in the forehead, and which appears to trigger her memories of her visits to the militiaman and the priest. The second statement is made by her father, when he comes to hurry her along with the packing: he says, 'Jetzt ist es wieder wie im Krieg' (*MFW*, 104). Windisch has used this turn of phrase before, particularly in response to the death of young Dietmar (*MFW*, 94), and on this occasion his remark is linked to the experience of leave-taking. While the intimation of Amalie's ordeal remains stark enough, the two framing statements remind us of what we know about her sexual self-awareness on the one hand, and of the mirroring of the older generation's experiences in hers on the other.

We have seen Windisch's sense of impotence in the face of authority express itself in frustrated rage at an earlier point, when he breaks a mirror by punching at the hallucinatory image of the militiaman (*MFW*, 85). That sense of impotence, and the growing awareness of what his daughter will have to do to obtain passports, give rise to the one occasion when we hear Windisch openly reproach his wife for her sexual behaviour at an earlier date. On that occasion it is his wife who tells him that he 'won't get far with his flour'; when he speaks of the shame in Amalie's sexual humiliation, it is his wife who insists that the practical value of obtaining passports outweighs any sense of shame in present circumstances; it is in this context that Windisch, after striking out at the shed door with his fist, accuses his wife of having developed the habit of peddling sex in the times of deprivation after the war (*MFW*, 74). This reproach is echoed at a later point. When wife and daughter together rebuke him for resorting to alcohol, he responds with 'whoring is healthier' (*MFW*, 88). The account of the wife's post-war experiences immediately follows that moment in the text.

Windisch, we are told, had returned to the village from captivity and had married Katharina because they had both lost their intended marriage partners in the war or its aftermath (*MFW*, 46 f.). She, together with other inhabitants of the village, had suffered a period of deportation in Russia. They had been required to work in mines and quarries. The experience of underground tunnels still has a traumatic effect on the tanner: when he goes to visit his son in the mountains he returns after only a few days because the memories awakened by passing through tunnels in the train have given him restless nights (*MFW*, 21 f.). Katharina's experiences during her five years in Russia are evoked directly, but with a narrative succinctness which throws into sharp relief their

significance at a distance of time. She had slept on an iron bed-
stead in a louse-infested shack. Her head had been shaven and her
scalp had become inflamed. Others in her contingent had frozen to
death on the lorry that took them to work each morning. At the
end of each winter she had exchanged an item of clothing for a
small amount of food. By the second winter she was sleeping with
a man in exchange for potatoes; by the fourth winter she was
sleeping with the local gravedigger, and when he died she
inherited the coat he had acquired from one of the corpses he had
buried (*MFW*, 89 ff.). What had driven her to do these things is
evoked in one recurrent image throughout this section of the text,
the image of her stomach as a hedgehog, with its spikes pressing
relentlessly into her consciousness. Katharina's experience is presented in terms which provide an immediate refutation of
Windisch's reproaches. By comparison with the brutally urgent
sense of her material need, however, her daughter's experience of
selling her body is left more open to interpretation. Amalie's recollection of that experience ends with a sharp pain in the belly, but
the objects associated with that pain are the high heels of the
white sandals which her mother had set out for her together with
her red dress, and which her father had seen her wearing at the
moment when he was struck by the way she walked (*MFW*, 82 f.,
103 f.). If Amalie's pressing pain is an indication of remorse or
revulsion, the white sandals are also a token both of her confident
assertion of her sexuality and of the calculated application of it in
which she has colluded with her mother.

Herta Müller's text is frank about the ultimately mysterious
nature of the impulses which determine human behaviour, and
does not attempt to account for them. No simple explanation is
offered, for instance, for the way that Amalie gathers glass objects
around her (*MFW*, 45 f.). Are they gifts from the children at the
kindergarten where she works, as she says they are, or does she
earn them in some other way? Are they somehow linked to the
tanner's son Rudi, whose personal connections in a glass factory
have helped provide his family with passports? Does Amalie's
mother share her enthusiasm for collecting glass as a possible way
of bribing officials, or are these women themselves simply avid for
prestigious possessions, as Windisch evidently supposes? Particular moments of sexual behaviour take on an obstinate significance
in the relations between characters, but they are not used as a
basis for psychological investigation as such. Windisch is haunted

by two such moments: by his wife's apparent act of self-gratifica-
tion on a thundery night (*MFW*, 17 f.), and by an incident when
Rudi had bitten Amalie's nipples when they were playing as
children (*MFW*, 40 f.). Both incidents are recounted with the same
matter-of-factness that characterizes the rest of the narrative, simply as past occurrences which come to colour perceptions of the
present. Other compulsive acts become part of the fabric of experience which the villagers share, and which enters into their sense
of conventional wisdom. The heat of summer has driven the carpenter's mother to behave in a curiously obsessive way. After
cooling a melon in the village well, she relentlessly devours it,
insisting that it is the only thing that will bring her relief. The
moment when she cuts the melon open is evoked as a murderous
act: 'Die Melone krachte. Es war ein Röcheln. Die Melone hatte im
Brunnen, hatte auf dem Küchentisch, bis ihre beiden Hälften
auseinanderfielen, noch gelebt' (*MFW*, 14). With the same knife
she has cut down a dahlia which had bloomed spectacularly in the
particular conditions of that summer. No one knows what she did
with the dahlia once she had cut it down, it simply disappeared;
but the villagers gathered for her funeral see the dahlia itself –
rather than what she did to it or to the melon – as a fatal sign or
apparition (*MFW*, 13). Another example of obsessive behaviour as
a harbinger of death is the case of old Frau Kroner, who harvests
the lime blossom from a neighbour's tree and spends a whole
winter drinking lime-blossom tea. The signs of impending death
are read in her face, and on this one occasion the text supplies an
interpretation of these signs as manifestations of a physiological
process, of a frailty regressing into youth and beyond: 'Ihr Gesicht
war jung. Das Jungsein war Schwäche. Wie man vor dem Sterben
jung wird, war das Gesicht. Wie man immer jünger und so jung
wird, bis der Körper bricht. Bis hinter die Geburt' (*MFW*, 43 f.).
But for Windisch, the moment of old Frau Kroner's death is
marked by the response of the external world, by the fact that the
owl has fallen silent (*MFW*, 42).

For this village community the owl is more than just a familiar
bird of prey, it is also believed to bring death to the house on
which it alights. That superstition is made explicit on the closing
pages of the work, when the night-watchman speaks of another
old woman driving the owl away from her house (*MFW*, 110). The
notion of an owl 'wishing a death' is also evoked when the tailor's
son Dietmar is killed. It was in the act of reaching out for a young

owl that a fellow soldier had let his rifle fall; and on hearing the news, Windisch's wife indirectly confirms the prevalence of the superstition when she says the owl couldn't help it, 'Da kann die Eule nichts dafür' (*MFW*, 94). This is a community in which a magical relationship with the natural world still has a strong hold and still generates its own remedies for supposedly unnatural occurrences. Windisch's memories include a story from pre-war days about an apple tree that was said to devour its own fruit. After the local bishop has been informed of what the villagers claim to have witnessed in the dead of night, the word comes back that the tree is not to be felled, as a normal tree would, but to be burned where it stands. Finally the charred trunk itself is reduced to ashes (*MFW*, 34 ff.). The community has experienced a moment of collective compulsion, a ritualized exorcism.

The most harrowing account of compulsive behaviour in this text is concerned with owls, and with an entire family history. It is recalled by Windisch as an instance of the inescapability of fate (*MFW*, 27 ff.). The tanner's grandmother had gone looking for her husband when he died young. She went looking for him in the fields one winter's evening, and froze to death. She left behind a three-year-old son, who became an obsessive carver of wood. When he carved the lime-tree behind the house into the figure of a naked woman, his wife took their child and left him. As the story goes on, the obsessions of earlier generations are visited upon the child. That child is the tanner, who grew up catching lizards and toads, took young owls from their nest in the church tower, fed them on lizards and toads until they grew large, then killed and stuffed them. Since the war his attic has filled up with stuffed owls, storks and blackbirds, as well as the skins of sheep and hares from roundabout. He is particularly remembered for having skinned a buck alive on the village square, and for his unheroic exploits in the war: 'schinden' is the activity in which he has become skilled, and by implication Windisch remembers him as a 'Menschenschinder', a brutal tormentor of his fellow human beings (*MFW*, 30). For the last two years there have been no owls nesting in the church tower because the tanner has killed the last one and stuffed it (*MFW*, 31). It is as if his obsessive urge to combat the supposed bringers of death is precisely what has turned him into a killer. But beyond its accumulation of suggestive imagery the text again refrains from psychological interpretation.

As a strategy for writing, Herta Müller's insistent focus on detail has been seen as consistent with the way German literary writing in Romania responded to a situation of intensified repression from the mid-1970s onwards.[3] In discussion at Swansea in 1996, she herself spoke of her concentration on detail as a conscious reaction to the blinkered models of Socialist Realism imposed on her generation, and on their perception of the world, at school.[4] In a contribution to the public discussion of utopias in 1994, she indicated how this aspect of her writing related to her development as a person, as well as to her conscious strategy as a writer. She reacted to the utopian language of socialism, and of religion, which had dominated the world in which she grew up, not by developing a counter-utopia, but by self-consciously focusing on the detail of what she experienced around her, as opposed to any sense of what it signified as a whole: 'Meine Einzelheiten hatten keine Gültigkeit, sie waren nicht ein Teil, sondern ein Feind des Ganzen. Wer wie ich damit anfing, in Einzelheiten zu leben, brachte das Ganze nie zusammen. Wer im Detail leben mußte, stellte nur Hürden auf für das Ganze' (*HS*, 59). Speaking on an earlier occasion about the way she wrote, she came up with a paradoxical formulation which has provided an understandable focus for critical attention to her work:[5] she spoke of a perception of the world which 'invented itself'. What she seemed to have in mind was the spontaneous formation in our memory of images fashioned out of our sensory responses to experiences, which come to stand for the entirety of those experiences: 'Ich merke an mir, daß nicht das am stärksten im Gedächtnis bleibt, was außen war, was man Fakten nennt. Stärker, weil wieder erlebbar im Gedächtnis, ist das, was auch damals im Kopf stand, das, was von innen kam, angesichts des Äußeren, der Fakten' (*TS*, 10). She goes on to mention the specific physical sensations associated with 'what came from inside': a sense of pressure under the ribs, a constriction of the throat, a racing of the pulse. These sensations, rather than anything so abstract as 'fear' or 'joy', are what create the traces out of which memory is truly constructed.

It may be the case that focus on detail came to have the significance for the young Herta Müller of a defensive mechanism, a preservation of individuality, in the face of an oppressive regime. In *Der Mensch ist ein großer Fasan auf der Welt* we find her systematically applying that principle in the evocation of the way the characters perceive their moments of confrontation or separation.

Sometimes the effect is to introduce a curious obliqueness into the presentation of a situation which might otherwise be all too readily perceived in terms of 'the facts': the narrative sequence, and the section heading, focuses, for example, on the fly that buzzes around at old Frau Kroner's funeral (*MFW*, 53 f.), or on the cabbage white butterfly which intrudes while Amalie is getting dressed up for her visit to the militiaman (*MFW*, 80 f.). Similarly, it is the trembling of the lettuce leaf on Amalie's fork to which our attention is drawn, rather than any more immediate sign of the growing mutual resentment within her family (*MFW*, 88), and the grass soup on which her mother survived her summers in Russia, rather than the facts which then emerge all the more brutally about the way she survived the winters (*MFW*, 89 ff.). More directly, it is the sensory awareness that characters have of owls or of glass objects which is overtly described in the text, rather than any abstracted sense of the fear or the expectation that is evidently associated with those things in their minds. For the nightwatchman, an owl that does not know its way around in the village *means* that young people, as opposed to the elderly and infirm, will die (*MFW*, 68). Glass remnants which Rudi has left after bribing an official with valuable artefacts are presented *as* the fingers, toes, lips, eyes of the lived experiences that glass objects have meant for him (*MFW*, 45). The frilly skirts of the dancer depicted on the standing vase which Amalie covets come to *stand for* the anticipation of erogenous display from a variety of perspectives: in Windisch's determination that no such vase should enter his house (*MFW*, 53), in his wife's envious comments on the skirts of a singer seen on television (*MFW*, 91 f.), and in Amalie's flirtation with Dietmar (*MFW*, 66), which is immediately preceded by the account of a gypsy girl lifting her skirts for money.

Remembered things are presented in this text as the external referents for the experiences out of which the characters' perceptions of their situations and of each other are constructed. The glass tear drop which Amalie carries with sentimental attachment is rejected by her father as something which 'makes people sad' (*MFW*, 104). It is the specific sights and feels of her sexual encounters that are recalled, rather than any summary judgement on the uses to which her sexuality is put. The focus on the minutiae of sensory experience creates an opportunity and a challenge for the reader, even if the author, in her interview with Brigid Haines and Margaret Littler, disclaims any interest in the reader as a participant in the construction of the text.[6] It is that focus on sensory detail which calls for an active, constructive response from the reader; and it is through the studied concentration on that order of experience that the text enables us to participate in an exploration of what the characters are like, rather than in any automatic assumptions about who they are.[7]

Notes

[1] The texts in *Niederungen* have been described as working on the boundary between sharply observed realistic depiction and the creation of surreal images. See Norbert Otto Eke, 'Augen/Blicke oder: Die Wahrnehmung der Welt in den Bildern. Annäherung an Herta Müller', in Norbert Otto Eke (ed.), *Die erfundene Wahrnehmung. Annäherung an Herta Müller* (Paderborn, Igel Verlag 1991), 7-21, here 14–17; also Claudia Becker, '"Serapiontisches Prinzip" in politischer Manier. Wirklichkeits- und Sprachbilder in *Niederungen*', in the same volume, 32–41.

[2] Herta Müller herself confirms in her interview with Brigid Haines and Margaret Littler that the image of the pheasant has these two dimensions: see this volume, 16.

[3] Eke, 'Augen/Blicke', 10 f.; see also Emmerich Reichrath, 'Vorwort', in *Reflexe II. Aufsätze, Rezensionen und Interviews zur deutschen Literatur in Rumänien* (Cluj-Napoca, 1984), 11 f.

[4] Swansea German Department video, 10 October 1996.

[5] See the contributions to Eke (ed.), *Die erfundene Wahrnehmung*.

[6] See this volume, 18.

[7] Herta Müller describes this distinction, too, as fundamental to her approach to writing: *HS*, 60.

5

Beyond Alienation:
The City in the Novels of Herta Müller and
Libuše Moníková

MARGARET LITTLER

In a *Guardian* interview on 4 November 1995 Salman Rushdie spoke of his love of cities as 'artificial man-made constructs', full of jumbled, hybridized people just like himself. Such sentiments may seem commonplace today, but in fact mark a shift away from one of the more traditional paradigms of gendered personifications of the city, in which the unruly forces of nature and the feminine are domesticated by the rational constraints of civilization. From medieval allegories of dragon-slaying and city-foundation, to the sexualization of urban space in the modernist city novel, an underlying structure of domination and subordination persists. It is implicit in Adorno and Horkheimer's critique of Enlightenment, in which the genesis of the rational bourgeois subject depends on the conquest of nature, mythology, and the feminine.[1] It is also present in Walter Benjamin's image of the *flaneur*, which transformed nineteenth-century Paris into the passive object of the male gaze. Whilst acknowledging the value of these interpretive models for the literature of European modernism, I will argue that they are no longer entirely appropriate to conceptualize the subjective experience of urban space in what may now be termed a 'postmetropolitan' age.[2] The novels I shall be discussing here belong to a time when the beleaguered subject of modernity has been displaced by a fragmented, discursively contested and sexually differentiated subject. It is also an age when, in the words of Daniel Bell, the organization of space has become 'the primary aesthetic problem of mid twentieth-century culture as the problem of time (in Bergson, Proust, and Joyce) was the primary aesthetic problem of the first decades of this century'.[3]

Given this 'change in sensibility',[4] it is surprising to see how frequently early twentieth-century models are still invoked in the

interpretation of contemporary representations of the city.[5] Yet
Walter Benjamin's fascination with the Paris arcades and urban
artefacts was motivated largely by nostalgia for a lost tradition,
underpinned and to some extent fuelled by the forward march of
modernization.[6] His essays on Baudelaire exude nostalgia for a
state of unalienated social integration and continuity of tradition.
It is thus not spatial relations *per se* and how they relate to identity
which interests him, so much as the proustian prompt to memory
which they afford. Yet nowhere is the impact of postmodernism
more apparent than in architecture and town planning, where the
rational functionalism of Mies van der Rohe, or Le Corbusier's
'modern machine for living' have given way to historical eclecti-
cism and the mixing of international and vernacular styles. Recent
writing on town planning demonstrates how it has overflowed its
disciplinary boundaries, as mechanistic models are replaced by
organic notions of the city as 'habitat', and architecture as the
extension of the collective and individual body.[7] Donatella
Mazzoleni, for example, influenced by R. D. Laing, writes of our
profound bodily investment in the buildings we inhabit, and the
city as only the largest of our 'body doubles', as likely to be the
site of identification as of alienation.[8]

Bearing this in mind, my interest in representations of the city
in novels of the 1980s is to see how the female subject relates to
public and private spaces, to consumerism and fashion, anonymity
and safety in the city. Above all I am concerned to illuminate how
the diversity of city life is experienced by subjects which are themselves dispersed and fragmented and may have no nostalgia for
some more wholesome past or for a coherent, integrated identity.
At the same time, my choice of the Czech author Libuše Moníková
and the Romanian-German writer Herta Müller will demonstrate
the subtle modalities produced by the historical location of their
postmodern subjects, situated as they are at the intersection of
gendered, linguistic, ethnic, and national identities.

The modernist paradigm: Benjamin and Simmel

Before turning to the novels, however, I would like to
acknowledge the work of two critics who have effectively invoked
Benjamin's notion of the *flaneur* in relation to the feminization of
the city. Sigrid Weigel's historical survey of constructions of the

city and 'the wild' in Western culture amply demonstrates how these intersect with discursive constructions of femininity. Woman is typically both *outside* the city as irrepressible nature, and *inside* it as civilized, conquered territory. This is linked to the organiz-ation of urban space into dual and opposing spheres, public/private, house/street, the city of the virgin/city of the whore. The solitary man in the crowd is confronted with the over-whelming organism of the city, and struggles to assert his identity by representing it, projecting onto its 'otherness' familiar and often mythological images.[9] Weigel attributes this heroic attitude of con-quest also to the *flaneur*, emphasizing the historical exclusion of women from this subject position: 'Einen weiblichen Flaneur kennt die Geschichte der Stadt nicht, denn die Straßen der Stadt waren lange Zeit dem Manne vorbehalten. Und als die Frauen begannen, sich als Subjekte die öffentlichen Plätze der Stadt zu erobern, als es für sie möglich wurde, allein durch die Straßen zu gehen, [. . .] da waren die Städte zur Flanerie schon nicht mehr geschaffen'.[10] Moreover, women's exclusion from *flaneur* status is not just a historical fact, but an essential condition of Benjamin's use of the term. His reading of Baudelaire draws parallels between the metropolitan masses, the ever-present crowd, and the feminine 'matter' to which the artist gives form.[11] Like the artist, the *flaneur* stands apart from the alienation of the crowds, enjoying a privi-leged, controlling gaze which holds the crisis of the modern world at bay.

Weigel does note an ambivalence of the *flaneur*, whose 'seduc-tion' by the city implies both passivity and control.[12] This passivity is emphasized by Elizabeth Wilson, who claims that to give one-self up thus to the city is a peculiarly feminine gesture.[13] Whilst I am less than happy with Wilson's willingness to equate submiss-iveness with femininity and her desire to 'claim' for female sub-jects the role of *flaneur*, her study does do a lot to dispel some of the myths about the inherent hostility of the urban environment for women, as well as to dismantle the binary opposition of public and private space on which it is based. She notes the freedoms afforded to women by city life, the ways in which the city 'norma-lises the carnivalesque aspects of life',[14] and sees urban life as based on the 'perpetual struggle between rigid, routinised order and pleasurable anarchy, the male-female dichotomy'.[15]

Wilson's more positive, emancipatory view of the city for women is more indebted to the sociologist Georg Simmel's writing

than to that of Benjamin. Writing in the first decades of this century, Simmel saw the positive side of urban anonymity as promot-
ing important forms of individualism, both diversity of lifestyle
and tolerance of eccentricity. His view of fashion also differed
from that of Benjamin; he saw it less as a form of capitalist exploitation and more as a possibility of self-representation. For Simmel
the modern city was 'one of those great historical structures in
which conflicting life-embracing currents find themselves with
equal legitimacy'.[16] His analysis of the 'metropolitan type', however, seems not so far removed from Benjamin's *flaneur*, in developing a reserved, intellectual detachment as protection against the
fluctuations and discontinuities of the city environment. Whilst
Simmel's work is remarkable for its analysis of conflict, exchange,
and the cultural diversity of urban life, his subject remains essentially a conscious, rational being, protecting its integrity from the
bombardment of stimuli from outside.

Nomadic Subjects: *Rosi Braidotti*

One of the liberating assertions of postmodern feminism is that
those things which represent a threat or a crisis for the dominant,
male subject of Western culture may be seen as an opportunity for
those traditionally denied subject status. Hence there emerges, for
example, from the potentially alienating effects of information
technology and cybernetic systems Donna Haraway's empowering
figure of the 'cyborg'; against the backdrop of trans-national mobility and the decline of the nation state Rosi Braidotti proposes a
new form of 'nomadic subject'. This implies a figure which resists
assimilation and enacts transitions without teleological purpose,
propelled forward only by desire. Identity is a retrospective notion, not built upon separation and domination, but made up of
the map of where one has already been, 'an inventory of traces'.[17]
She defines it as follows: 'The nomad does not stand for homeless-
ness, or compulsive displacement; it is rather a figuration for the
kind of subject who has relinquished all idea, desire, or nostalgia
for fixity. This figuration expresses the desire for an identity made
of transitions, successive shifts, and coordinated changes, without
and against an essential unity'.[18] Braidotti sees urban localities
such as departure lounges, railway stations, check-in halls as

'oases of nonbelonging' which provide the ideal setting for her 'nomads'.

Whether construed as the product of modernity or the hallmark of postmodernity, there can be no doubt that the decline of classical rationality has opened up radically new notions of subjectivity, occupying a spectrum of degrees of fixity. That proposed by Moníková is culturally non-assimilated, but lays claim to an identity based on nation state and cultural revivalism, whilst Müller constructs what I would call a 'city nomad' who rejects the binary logic on which modern conceptions of the city were based; in whom chaotic urban diversity is intrinsic to her subjectivity, rather than being that against which she defines herself. While both authors' work is autobiographically coloured, it is perhaps no coincidence that the writer who departs more radically from notions of rational subjectivity is also the more stylistically innovative and less constrained by conventional structures of meaning.

Libuše Moníková: Eine Schädigung *and* Pavane für eine verstorbene Infantin

Libuše Moníková, born in Prague in 1945, lived in Germany from 1971 until her death in 1998, and chose to publish in German, although not her first language, because of the distance it afforded her to write with precision: she could never take the language for granted. As Brigid Haines has demonstrated, her most insistent concern is to reclaim the twentieth-century history of Czechoslovakia from the dominant historical narratives in which her compatriots are the habitual and compliant victims.[19] *Eine Schädigung* (1981) illustrates both her feminism and her Czech identity: as the story of the rape of a young woman by a policeman, whom she then kills in self-defence, it can be read as a critique of male violence against women, and also as a story of the symbolic 'rape' of Czechoslovakia in 1968. The novel is dedicated to Jan Palach, and the protagonist's name 'Jana' is a feminization of his name.

The scene of the crime is in the oppressive atmosphere of an unnamed Eastern European city which keeps its citizens under surveillance from sinister towers. Jana is a student who works a night shift on the city's trams, and is raped on her way home one morning. The fact that she strikes back at her attacker has been criticized by Regula Venske as a mere reversal of the victim–oppressor relationship.[20] However, the rape and murder take place at the start of the novel, so the murder need not be seen as a positive solution, but rather as the logical outcome of the city's culture of violence and anonymity. The violation of her body sharpens Jana's awareness both of her own sex and of the city's hostility, and she sees the crowds transformed into an undifferentiated, faceless mass. The violence begins with the assault on the buildings of pollution from the streets, and is transmitted to fearful pedestrians dodging the traffic. As Jana observes this there is both horror and pity for the city in her gaze, as she looks at the ravaged façades of *fin-de-siècle* architecture:

Passanten laufen ungeschickt, schreckhaft zwischen den Straßenbahnen und der Fahrbahn –, von oben sieht sie die Gefährlichkeit. [. . .] Die Feindseligkeit hebt sich vom Pflaster mit den Abgasen der Fahrzeuge bis zu den höchsten Fenstern in dem Sezessionsverputz. Die Fronten mit Engeln über den Haustüren, mit blauen Mosaiken zwischen den Etagen und mit Ornamenten, die sich den Erkern entlang ziehen, sind schwarz von der täglichen Zerstörung.

[. . .] Die Paradehäuser der Jahrhundertwende mit ihrer verschnörkelten Größe stehen starr neben dem Chaos, sie übersehen es und verbinden sich mit der Landschaft, die auf der anderen Seite beginnt, wo hinter einer Sperre von Gebüsch ein großer Park liegt, der zu ihrer Zeit gepflanzt worden war.[21]

The *Jugendstil* architecture evoked here was a decorative, unruly branch of modernism, contrasting with the abstract, universalizing modernism which was appropriated by European fascism later in the twentieth century.[22] It is the strand of modernist architecture in which David Harvey detects continuities with postmodernism, with its interest in local determinism, vernacular styles, and identity of place. In Jana's lasting attachment to the city there is an unmistakable element of identification, in spite of the violence that inhabits its streets. Indeed, an opposition is set up between the old medieval town centre and the turn-of-the-century *Jugendstil* on the one hand, and the ugly concrete suburbs and the sinister modern towers on the other. Jana feels protective towards the old town, threatened with destruction;[23] her relationship to the city's architecture is clearly more complex than one of alienation in the face of the shock effect of urban life. Indeed, most of the novel is concerned with Jana's attempts to find a way of inhabiting the city after her rape. She declines the offer of refuge with Mara, an artist who lives a peripatetic life in a houseboat on the city's canals, constantly moving on from one prohibition to the next. Jana finds solace instead in back-street cinemas and in 'unauffindbare[n] Plätze[n] inmitten der Stadt'.[24]

Immediately after her rape she does perceive the city crowds in almost Benjaminian terms, as a hostile and threatening mass:

> Es ergriff sie das heiße Wogen entgegengestemmter Schultern, schleudernder Arme und schwerfälliger Füße. Es waren nicht viele Mädchen unter den Entgegenkommenden und es war nicht die Verschiedenheit der Gesichter, die sie hinderte, Verbindung aufzunehmen, sondern ihre Einheitlichkeit. Neben kleinen einzelnen Häßlichkeiten bewahrten sie die Haupthäßlichkeit gemeinsam – einen stumpfen, erhabenen Zug um den Mund, der kalt und schlaff in die Wangen zog.[25]

She is also particularly disturbed by the complicity of the women in their slavish adherence to fashion, which emphasizes their sexual vulnerability. In a highly unflattering description of 1970s flares and platform shoes, she notes:

> Die Mädchen wankten mit schiebenden Schritten vorwärts, in den Zwangshosen kaum beweglich, mit erschütternder Überzeugungskraft ihre physische Ohnmacht demonstrierend. Wollten sie vergewaltigt werden, auf der Straße umgestoßen und benützt werden, da sie sich schon im voraus jeder Widerstandsmöglichkeit entledigt hatten? Niemand müßte sie fesseln.[26]

In the intense anxiety of her traumatized state, fashion is here unequivocally a means of oppression, not an opportunity for playful feminine masquerade.

However, instead of a reproduction of the familiar modernist paradigm, Jana's disorientation in the city could be understood in terms of the potentially productive crisis of post-metropolitan existence described by Mazzoleni; one consequence of technological advance being the expansion of the city's dimensions far beyond the perceptive capacities of its inhabitants, in particular their sense of sight. The result is a challenge to the scopophilia of Western conceptions of space: 'In the metropolis there is no longer panorama (the vision of all), because its body overflows beyond the horizon. In the metropolitan aesthetic the eye fails in its role as an instrument of total control at a distance; once more the ears, and then the nose and skin, acquire an equal importance'.[27] Hence it is significant that Jana resolves to remain in the city, gradually reinstating her numbed senses of smell, touch, hearing, and taste, in an attempt to overcome her paranoid fear; the senses of taste and smell help to render the visual impressions of the city streets less threatening:

> Dann konnte sie nicht widerstehen, als von einer Bäckerei ihr der frische Geruch entgegenzog, ein süßer warmer Strom, der nach Vanille roch. Sie kaufte sich einen Kuchen, und während sie ihn aß, veränderte sich die Straße durch den Geschmack und durch das Gefühl der Sättigung, sie rückte weiter, wurde fremder und klarer, und die Menschen rückten mit.
>
> Jana betrachtete sie auf dem Hintergrund der Straßenorganisation, der Verteilung der Läden, der Grünanlagen, der Sonne, und suchte nach Übereinstimmungen, die genauso zufällig waren wie die Reihenfolge der Geschäfte.
>
> [. . .] das Spiel befreite Jana. Sie empfand keine gezielte Feindlichkeit mehr, keine Bedrohung, sie konzentrierte sich auf ihre Wahrnehmungen.[28]

Moníková's second novel *Pavane für eine verstorbene Infantin* (1983) is more personally autobiographical, as the story of a young Czech woman academic working in Germany, but cities again form an important subjective dimension. Francine Pallas teaches German literature at a North German university, travelling occasionally to Göttingen, but also describing journeys to Paris and Prague. Her crisis is more complex than that of Jana, involving her marginalization both as a woman in academia, and as a Czech national in Germany, and her problematic relationship to her own cultural heritage.[29] Her experience of German towns is consistent with her non-German identity: their anonymity and diversity appeal to her (her neighbours are a mixture of non-assimilated Turks, Silesians, and trendy liberal Germans), and she resists all attempts made to impose on her alien patterns of behaviour. She is particularly irritated by the Germans' patronizing ignorance of foreign cultures, and especially by their shortening of the name of her country to 'die Tschechei', and their expectation that Czechs will speak German. Although she despises the passivity of the Czechs, and avoids associating with them abroad, she is constantly outraged on their behalf, and that of all minorities who suffer discrimination in Germany.

The cumulative stresses of Francine's permanent state of non-belonging manifest themselves in a physical symptom: a pain in her hip which causes her to limp. She eventually buys and starts to use a wheelchair, acting out a disability which renders visible her sense of difference. This has been interpreted as an example of 'Körper-Sprache', a physical symptom not repressed but positively played out to materialize her outsider-status.[30] However, in the light of Moníková's intertexts, I see it rather as a self-imposed limitation which facilitates Francine's establishment of an identity in the city.[31] Her pain had begun in Paris, where she is irritated by the 'Paris myth', and by the fact that her friend Geneviève has to live in poverty there because rents are so exorbitantly high. She cannot help but object to the pollution and corruption she sees everywhere, prompting from Geneviève the comment: 'Du kommst in ein fremdes Land und fängst sofort an, alles umzu-krempeln, statt dich anzupassen'.[32] The injunction to 'adapt' pro-vokes Francine to adopt a wilfully asymmetrical gait, quite differ-ent from the measured steps of Ravel's Pavane in the title.

Francine experiences life in Germany as a sort of simulacrum; the novel opens with a series of unconnected TV images, prompt-ing her to reflect on how often she sees literary and filmic paral-lels with her own experience, as if someone had lived everything before her. This is conveyed stylistically in the many unattributed italicized quotations in the text. But within this 'textual universe', she retains a strong class consciousness and awareness of her own Czech origins. So, for example, when teaching Virginia Woolf's *A Room of One's Own* in a women's writing seminar, she is critical of Woolf as a woman whose *class* enabled her to enjoy the privileges of a *flaneur*. Nor can she identify with the radical feminism of her West German students, all bent on turning her seminar into a consciousness-raising meeting, and projecting onto Francine the role of authority against which to rebel. She wants the students to read Woolf critically, challenging her claims to speak for 'woman-kind' when she was so untypical of the mass of female experience: 'Virginia Woolf gerät das Elend auf den Straßen Londons zum Stadtkolorit. Sie spricht von der Ungerechtigkeit der Frauenaus-bildung, von ihrer ökonomischen Abhängigkeit und ist gleichzeitig von Kindheit an gewöhnt, Hauspersonal zu haben; bis zuletzt hatte sie zwei weibliche Bedienstete'.[33] For Francine it is Woolf's madness and suicide which are more significant for feminism than her analysis of the female condition, but the students just embrace her uncritically as a champion of their cause.

Her relationship to the city of Prague remains strong, even when her personal contacts there are fraught with conflict (as with her sister). Through her memories of student days and through Kafka's writing she retains a deep attachment to the city. This is no postmodern metropolitan consciousness, but rather a fantasy of origins; in mythological passages she identifies with the heathen princess Libuše who is said to have founded Prague, and with the poor, dishevelled Bohemian lion: 'Ich bin am Ort meines Ursprungs; wir stehen uns gegenüber, am Ausgang unserer vergeblichen Geschichte – die Fürstin und das Wappentier'.[34] She invents for Bohemia a more glorious history, incorporating Shakespeare's topographical error of giving it a coastline (in *The Winter's Tale*), the return to Prague of Kafka's manuscripts, dispersed in various foreign archives (including the Bodleian Library, Oxford), the return of territories lost to the Ukraine, and the introduction of a compulsory requirement for all tourists to speak Czech. Prague, with its founding myth and its place in European literature, is emblematic for Czech identity. It is the focus of her desire to reclaim Czech history and restore pride and integrity to the Czech people.[35]

Her ambivalence towards Kafka is symptomatic of her relationship to her Czech identity. Particularly insensed by the passive suffering of Kafka's victims, she devotes herself more and more to the 're-writing of literary fates', setting out to rewrite *Das Schloß* in an attempt to redeem the family of Barnabas. On the one hand, she identifies with Kafka and loves his work, but she cannot accept his characters' unquestioned subjection to the judgements of a usually incomprehensible authority. The novel is strewn with references to his stories, including the story about the Tower of Babel 'Das Stadtwappen', which Francine takes to be about Prague, firstly because of its cultural and linguistic diversity, but also as a city founded on the death wish of its own destruction.[36] Prague's significance in the novel is intimately bound up with its status as capital of the Czech nation; thus metropolitan, cultural, and national identity are ultimately conflated in Moníková's novel.

Herta Müller, Reisende auf einem Bein

If the city of Prague is coextensive with a sense of national identity for Moníková, Herta Müller opposes city and state in her novel *Reisende auf einem Bein* (1989). In her autobiographical essays, Müller contrasts the power of state control in the Romanian village in which she grew up with the relative freedom she experienced when she moved to the city to study and work. Paradoxically it was in the apparent remoteness of the rural village that norms of behaviour were more rigorously obeyed and the status quo was more tyrannically upheld.[37] She also noticed that it was only in the city that madness and misfits were tolerated: 'Diese Irregewordenen durften in den Straßen der Stadt wohnen. Die Diktatur kümmerte sich nicht um sie' (*HS*, 95). Madness was both a symptom of dictatorship and a tolerated form of eccentricity in the city; it was perceived by the citizens as proof of their own normality. When Müller herself had refused to inform for the *Securitate*, lost her job and became semi-criminalized, she too had been considered 'mad' by former colleagues.

The female protagonist of *Reisende auf einem Bein* has left 'das andere Land' with its border patrols and radar screens, initially to be with her German lover, Franz (a student in Marburg), but even when their relationship breaks down, she remains in West Berlin and applies for German citizenship. As a German-speaking Romanian, like Müller herself, she is doubly alienated on arrival in Berlin to hear her 'mother-tongue' being spoken by these German 'foreigners'. She remains a perpetual visitor in Berlin, 'Ausländerin im Ausland' (*RB*, 61), not homeless, but resisting assimilation in every way. She is placed at first in an 'Asylantenheim', because there is no room in the hostel for 'Aussiedler', those ethnic Germans from Eastern Europe who, until the early 1990s, enjoyed an almost automatic right to German citizenship. She observes the poor refugees rummaging in cheap shoe-baskets outside shops to find matching pairs. Shoes become a metaphor for identity, the resemblance between them analogous to that between the real and the imaginary subject, a unity with an inbuilt distance:

> Irene hatte gesehn, wie die Männer und Frauen den einen, passenden Schuh gefunden hatten. Wie sie ihn über den Kopf hielten mit der einen Hand. Mit der anderen Hand weiter wühlten, im Haufen der auseinandergerissenen Paare.

Und diese Entfernung blieb, von einem Schuh zum andern. Sie wuchs
hinter den Rücken. Schloß auch die Schultern ein. Auch in den Augen
stand diese Entfernung. (*RB*, 29 f.)

Somewhat reminiscent of Moníková's limping Francine, Irene's
step is described as light and uneven, but more like Braidotti's
nomadic subject, Irene is propelled through the city streets by
desire: 'Irene spürte die Haut in ihren Kniekehlen. Und Takte. Es
war Erregung, die Irene durch die Straßen trieb. Die Schritte waren ungleichmäßig, aber leicht' (*RB*, 75).

Irene had left home 'auf den Strümpfen', bringing no fixed
identity. She is unable to identify with photographs of herself, she
has a liking for collage and is fascinated by the snippets of other
lives which she constantly brushes up against in the street (*RB*, 54
f.). She occasionally experiences quite disturbing spatial dislocation, but mainly positively enjoys the strangeness, the fact that her
body cannot adjust to its new location, for example she laughs
when she falls out of bed because her bed was located differently
in relation to the room in her bedroom at home (*RB*, 120).

If Moníková depicts a metropolitan subject in crisis, Müller's
novel suggests a more positive reconceptualization of the city as
'habitat', an extension of the bodily experience of space. This can
be seen in Irene's relation to bodily gestures, fashion and clothing,
and to the objects which surround her. In *Der Teufel sitzt im Spiegel*
Müller writes that the gesture of touching oneself is a way of
securing a sense of integrity in the face of our essential fragmentation (*TS*, 83).[38] She also writes that the gestures which accompany
speech indicate both the inadequacies of language and our desire
to reach out beyond our body boundaries to others: 'Und, was
bringt uns *dazu*, all die *Gesten* zu tun, wenn wir in Worten reden.
Vielleicht wollen wir jenseits der Haut ausdehnen, was uns mit
dem anderen verbindet' (*TS*, 83). In the context of Mazzoleni's
notion of urban 'habitat', the primacy of objects and the importance of gestures in Müller's writing can be seen as non-verbal
means whereby we extend our 'proxemic sphere'.[39]

This is certainly the case for Irene, whose gestures aim at an
intimacy with others and her environment based on an intense
proximity, not appropriation. Franz, in contrast, tolerates no
infringement of his body boundaries, to the extent that his gestures have become fixed and predictable, making him appear like
an old man rather than ten years Irene's junior: 'Irene sah wieder,

daß Franz zu viele Gesten hatte, die sich nie mehr änderten. Es waren, wie bei alten Leuten, verbissene, für immer festgelegte Gesten. Sie waren verhärtet und machten ihn alt' (*RB*, 125).

The relationship to objects described by Müller has nothing to do with materialism in a capitalist sense. When she reflects on the intolerable dislocation of asylum-seekers in Germany, for example, they are seen as lacking the privilege to inhabit their environment unquestioningly. It is explicitly 'keine Frage des Eigentums, sondern eine des Sich-Investieren-Könnens' (*KB*, 53). Thus Irene's dismay at the relatively sparsely furnished German apartments is based on Müller's experience in Romania, and at the same time expresses an extension of identity beyond subjective boundaries. In Ceauşescu's Romania surrounding oneself with familiar objects was the only security possible against the all-pervasive power of the state. She writes in *Der Teufel sitzt im Spiegel* of the relief of waking up among well-known objects which made no demands, but offered stability and an extension of the body: 'ich konnte atmen, konnte weg von der Haut: Überall Gegenstände, wo die Haut zu Ende war' (*TS*, 91). Objects in Müller's work often have ritual functions, never simply surrounding her characters, but inhabiting them and impacting on their lives. Thus when Irene goes to view a flat in Berlin, the rooms pass through her consciousness, rather than being the passive objects of her gaze: 'Dann ging ein Flur durch sie hindurch. Dann eine Küche. Dann ein Bad. Dann ein Zimmer. Alles leere Wände' (*RB*, 38). Similarly, when falling asleep in her new flat, Irene experiences architectural space as the concretization and extension of her body:

> Irene spürte die Wärme des Rückens, die Wärme des Betts, die Wärme der Kleider und die Wärme der Haut.
> Jede Wärme war anders.
> Der Rand der Decke lag um den Hals. Irene fühlte sich wie begraben.
> Ihre Lider wurden länger. Reichten für das ganze Gesicht.
> Für das ganze Zimmer reichten Irenes Lider.
> Langsam schlossen sie sich.
> In Schattenstreifen verwandelt wie Jalousien. (*RB*, 42)

Like objects, items of clothing enter into a relationship with their wearers, as in the case of Thomas's compulsive shirt-buying, which is represented in terms of a love-affair in which he is seduced and temporarily transformed by the shirt, as Müller herself has commented: 'Das Hemd ist selbstständig, es nimmt keine

Eigenschaften an. Das Hemd wird nicht wie Thomas. Thomas wird wie das Hemd. Thomas wird zum Gegenstand des Hemdes' (*TS*, 99).[40] Thomas's libidinal investment in the shirt corresponds to Mazzoleni's view that 'clothes are not simply a covering or a disguise, they are also a profound investment of the body'.[41]

In contrast with Moníková's Jana, fashion is experienced by Irene as both manipulative and potentially liberating – a fund of new identities, all provisional and holding the excitement of the new: 'Irene wünschte sich mehrere Körper, um die Kleider aus den Schaufenstern zu tragen. Und Geld, um die Kleider zu kaufen. Und, daß man die Kleider nicht kaufen mußte, nur borgen, sich müde tragen an ihnen, einige Tage' (*RB*, 75). Rather than an instrument of manipulation or compensation, then, fashion may be seen here as a medium of female identity assertion, albeit a temporary and negotiable identity.[42]

As Irene watches women's fashions in the street, she finds herself cast in the role of male voyeur, and is aware of the fetish character of women's clothes. She sees 'Beine für Männer. Beine mit Schlingen. Sie fingen Blicke ein. Auch Irenes Blicke fingen sie ein' (*RB*, 75). Whilst aware of being the object as well as the subject of this gaze, Irene is also aroused by the somatic experience of the streets, as we have seen. The feet, as the site of both fetishism and identity, are also the point of contact with the city. Thus the footsteps of the refugees from the 'Asylantenheim' make no sound (*RB*, 29), and when Irene describes homesickness, it is as a physical sensation, 'Wenn man mal zu leicht und mal zu schwer ist auf den Straßen' (*RB*, 79).

The city poses a challenge to the conscious subject's integrity, but in a way which is experienced as liberating rather than threatening, and recalls Mazzoleni's psychoanalytical model. In place of a threatening 'loss of self', she sees the postmodern metropolitan experience as a site of re-connection to 'an "ancient" state of pre-separation, of prevarication, but also of the increasing nutrition of the I, and so of the loss of the I's borders to a vital mass without surroundings'. Metropolitan life consists of 'a "knot" of spatial experience, a point at which the most elementary distinction of space – the distinction between "inside" and "outside", which is the very distinction between "I" and "the world" – grows weaker'.[43] This is a conception of the city as 'a habitat without a "somewhere else"',[44] as distinct from an entity defined by its separation from an 'other' beyond its limits.

The city surrounds Irene almost like a semiotic chora (Kristeva), at its most intrusive when consciousness loses its hold. Thus, when she concentrates her thoughts on Franz, the city is still and objectified, giving her an 'äußere Sicherheit' (*RB*, 62). Nevertheless this stability is only provisional, she cannot control the flux of the city for long: 'Wenn der Schädel stillstand, wuchs der Asphalt. Wenn der Asphalt stillstand, wuchs die Leere im Schädel. Mal fiel die Stadt über Irenes Gedanken her. Mal Irenes Gedanken über die Stadt' (*RB*, 63). Müller herself relates this passage in the novel to the unrealized potential inherent in all human experience. Her characters are not agents in a static, passive environment, but inhere in a world which holds open multiple unexpected possibilities. This is signalled stylistically by short, open-ended sentences, in the attempt to capture in language the moment of perception, that moment of signification which exceeds every utterance: 'Das Gesagte muß behutsam sein, mit dem, was nicht gesagt wird. [. . .] Das, was mich einkreist, seine Wege geht, beim Lesen, ist das, was zwischen den Sätzen fällt und aufschlägt, oder kein Geräusch macht. Es ist das Ausgelassene' (*TS*, 19).

Thus the city is experienced – at least by Irene – as an extension of her own body and psyche, not as that against which she defines her own subjectivity. Indeed, the concept of an identity imposed by an abstract entity such as the nation state is anathema to Irene. In this she echoes Müller's own experience of growing up under the threefold coercion of a patriarchal family, an obligatory German minority identity, and the overarching totalitarian state.[45] Like Müller, on her arrival in Berlin Irene does not fit any of the categories on the pre-printed immigration forms, being both an ethnic German and a political refugee. This merely confirms the fluidity of her identity, and as her relationship with Franz deteriorates, she reflects on the tension between them in terms of a 'Stadt'/'Staat' opposition, in which Irene rejects any national identity in favour of identification with the city. Franz is irritated by his own disorientation in Berlin and implicitly blames her: 'Franz fand keinen Parkplatz in der Straße. Er zerrte am Lenkrad und beschimpfte die Stadt. Er beschimpfte die Stadt, in der Irene lebte, und sah Irene an'. He has recourse to a notion of fatherland: 'Da sich die Stadt verweigerte, brauchte er den Staat. [. . .] Ein Staat. Und Franz und mittendrin der Umfang seiner Rippen'. Irene is sceptical about this egocentric notion of national identity, having experienced the negative aspects of national identity in a dictatorship, and she asks, 'Wo trägst du es, dein Vaterland, wenn es plötzlich gegen deinen Willen da ist?' (*RB*, 124).

Müller's most significant intertext is Italo Calvino's *Invisible Cities* (1972), in which the Venetian envoy Marco Polo reports to the Tartar emperor Kublai Khan about the cities of his empire. The descriptions are to reassure the emperor of the extent and glory of his dominion, but it turns out that they resist any such appropriation.[46] Calvino's novel suggests the impossibility of ever knowing and conquering the 'other', represented here in the form of cities, all of which have female names. Like Berlin in Müller's novel, the cities all resist male conquest, the locality of place asserts its difference from the abstract space of fatherland/empire. The extract from Calvino's novel quoted in the text is also indicative of the distance inherent in Irene's identity:

> Irene is a name for a city in the distance, and if you approach, it changes. For those who pass it without entering, the city is one thing; it is another for those who are trapped by it and never leave. There is the city where you arrive for the first time; and there is another city which you leave never to return. Each deserves a different name; perhaps I have already spoken of Irene under other names; perhaps I have spoken only of Irene.[47]

This expresses Franz's frustration at not being able to possess Irene, in the same way that he appropriates the spaces he inhabits, so that when Irene visits Marburg she finds him everywhere, limiting her freedom, imposing thoughts of him on her (*RB*, 143). Kublai Khan's imperialist aim is described as a dematerialization as well as decoding of the cities of his empire. He wants to discover the model for all possible cities, the 'norm' from which all other cities may be deduced. Marco Polo opposes to this the antithesis, the view that cities are like dreams, resistant to all manifest interpretation. His ideal city is 'a city made only of exceptions, exclusions, incongruities, contradictions'.[48] This accords with Müller's view that the city is a promiscuous, pluralist realm, in which Irene occupies a precarious position as a traveller and would-be inhabitant, unable ever to take the city for granted; she is a 'Reisende auf einem Bein und auf dem anderen Verlorene' (*RB*, 92).

In contrast, those who truly inhabit the city enjoy a physical intimacy with it and can treat it as an easy extension of their own

bodies (*RB*, 138 f.). Irene starts to envy them and to regret the dislocation and distance which reduce her to a *flaneur*; she longs to
inhabit the city in the same way, not merely to watch its life
unfold: 'In diesen Augenblicken wußte Irene, daß ihr Leben zu
Beobachtungen geronnen war. Die Beobachtungen machten sie
handlungsunfähig' (*RB*, 139). By the end of the novel, when she
has been granted German citizenship and has decided to stay in
Berlin, she finds it increasingly difficult to differentiate between
those who are 'Reisende in dünnen Schuhen', and 'Bewohner mit
Handgepäck' (*RB*, 166).

The fact that Müller's subsequent two novels both return to Romanian settings and depict a darker view of the possible subject
positions open to her characters is perhaps indicative that a pluralist society is a prerequisite for the postmodern experience of city
life so vividly evoked in *Reisende auf einem Bein*. The protagonists
of *Der Fuchs war damals schon der Jäger* (1992) all live in Timişoara,
where they endure constant invasions of their private space by the
Securitate. Nevertheless, the city is still the place where subversive
concerts can be held and dissent is possible. When Paul and Adina
flee arrest and take refuge in the village home of Liviu, a
schoolteacher in the country, they are unable even to leave the
house for fear of discovery. As Liviu's wife observes: 'Hier weiß
jeder, was sein Nachbar vorgestern gegessen hat [. . .], was er
kauft und verkauft und wieviel Geld er hat' (*FJ*, 260). The city, by
contrast, has its wildernesses, such as the woodland behind the
hospital where Paul works. It is an overgrown tree-nursery, older
than the hospital and neighbouring housing, and represents the
'frayed edge' of the city, where illicit lovemaking and children's
unauthorized wild play take place among the tangled under-
growth. Even in the dictatorship, that which is excluded from
civilization hovers on the fringes, always threatening to return.

In *Herztier* (1994), a novel about friendship, love, death and
betrayal in Ceauşescu's Romania, even this degree of freedom is
not afforded by the city. Indeed, as one of the four friends at the
centre of the novel, Georg, asserts: 'In einer Diktatur kann es keine
Städte geben' (*HT*, 52). When the female protagonist first arrives
in her university town to study, she notices that all the other
incomers carry their home villages in their faces. This breaking
down of the symbolic town/country divide belies the Party propaganda about the rural areas being as prosperous as the city, and
exposes the equally backward state of arable and industrial

production. The only inhabitants of the city who do not live in constant fear are the homeless and insane: 'Sie hatten die Angst vertauscht mit dem Wahn' (*HT*, 49). As in her other novels, objects such as the wooden 'Hühnerqual' given to the narrator by Georg, have a talismanic significance, given the extreme insecurity of their dissident existence. Fear and complicity produce a strong ethical bond between the friends, one which on the one hand suggests a more humanist and anchored view of the subject, and on the other obviates the possibility of individual agency, as the actions of each of them implicate the others: 'Du bist nicht nur du', as Edgar tells the narrator (*HT*, 206). Thus even in this very bleak depiction of life under totalitarianism there is an enforced renegotiation of the boundaries of the self.

To return to Salman Rushdie's words with which I opened, of the novels I have discussed, Herta Müller's comes the closest to depicting such a 'postmodern' experience of the self as diffuse and contradictory, at home in the diversity of urban life. The non-assimilation of Moníková's Francine Pallas is motivated more by a desire to recreate a more honourable Czech identity, and is closer to Braidotti's category of the 'exile' than to that of the 'nomad', remaining in a marginalized and hostile relationship to the host country.[49] While Herta Müller's 'Aussiedler' status affords her a certain narrative freedom to experiment with a spectrum of subject positions, Moníková's voluntary exile entailed (at least in her pre-1989 work) the continued assertion of national and cultural origins.[50] Neither of them articulates a simple nostalgia for unalienated, sexually undifferentiated subjectivity, nor do they represent the city as a necessarily hostile environment. However, the contrasts between them demonstrate, in my view, the locatedness of all contemporary subjectivity, which, for women, is a constant negotiation between the *theoretical* affirmation of fragmentation, mobility and difference on the one hand, and the *political* need to occupy positions of real subjective agency, on the other.

Notes

[1] Sigrid Weigel, *Topographien der Geschlechter. Kulturgeschichtliche Studien zur Literatur* (Reinbek, Rowohlt, 1990), 115–229.

[2] See Donatella Mazzoleni, 'The city and the imaginary', *New Formations*, 11 (1990), 91–104, here 100.

[3] See David Harvey, *The Condition of Postmodernity* (Oxford, Blackwell, 1990), 201; also Madan Sarup, *An Introductory Guide to Poststructuralism and Postmodernism* (Hemel Hempstead, Harvester Wheatsheaf, 1988), 146.

[4] Andreas Huyssens, 'Mapping the postmodern', *New German Critique*, 33 (1984), 5–52, here 8.

[5] See for example Sigrid Weigel's cultural-historical exploration: 'Wildnis und Stadt', in Weigel, *Topographien der Geschlechter*, 115–229; Elizabeth Wilson, *The Sphinx in the City: Urban Life, the Control of Disorder, and Women* (London, Virago, 1991); and Maria Kublitz-Kramer's fascinating study of Moníková, Müller, and Anne Duden, 'Die Freiheiten der Straße. Stadtläuferinnen in neueren Texten von Frauen', in Friedmar Apel, Maria Kublitz-Kramer and Thomas Steinfeld, *Kultur in der Stadt* (Paderborn, Universität Paderborn, 1993), 15–36.

[6] Susan Buck-Morss underlines the contradictory impulses underlying Benjamin's 'Passagenwerk', which was seeking on the one hand to reveal the unconscious secrets of a 'dreaming collective', much as Proust had uncovered his own forgotten history, and on the other hand was bound in fascination for the international style of modern architecture: the arcades were the 'hallmark of the modern metropolis'. Susan Buck-Morss, *The Dialectics of Seeing: Walter Benjamin and the Arcades Project* (Cambridge/Mass; London, MIT Press, 1989), 39.

[7] Mazzoleni, 'The city and the imaginary', 94.

[8] Ibid., 97.

[9] Weigel, *Topographien der Geschlechter*, 193 f.

[10] Sigrid Weigel, 'Flaneurin in der Welt der Schrift. Spuren Benjaminischer Lektüre in den Texten von Ginka Steinwachs', in Sonia Nowoselsky-Müller (ed.), *ein mund von welt. Ginka Steinwachs. Text//s//orte//n* (Bremen, Zeichen und Spuren, 1989), 62–9, here 66.

[11] Benjamin describes the Paris crowds in Baudelaire's work as follows: 'Es ist die Geistermenge der Worte, der Fragmente, der Versanfänge, mit denen der Dichter in den verlassenen Straßenzügen den Kampf um die poetische Beute ausficht'. Walter Benjamin, 'Über einige Motive bei Baudelaire', in Walter Benjamin, *Gesammelte Schriften*, 1.2, eds. Rolf Tiedemann and Hermann Schweppenhäuser (Frankfurt, Suhrkamp, 1974), 605–58, here 618.

[12] Weigel, *Topographien der Geschlechter*, 175.

[13] Wilson, *The Sphinx in the City*, 25.

[14] Ibid., 7.

[15] Ibid., 7 f.

[16] Georg Simmel, 'The metropolis and mental life' (1903), in Georg Simmel, *On Individuality and Social Forms: Selected Writings*, ed. Donald N. Levine (Chicago; London, Chicago University Press, 1971), 324–39, here 339.

[17] Rosi Braidotti, *Nomadic Subjects: Embodiment and Sexual Difference in Contemporary Feminist Theory* (New York, Columbia University Press, 1994), 14.

[18] Ibid., 22.

[19] Brigid Haines, '"New places from which to write histories of

peoples": power and the personal in the novels of Libuše Moníková', *German Life and Letters*, 49 No. 4 (1996), 501–12.

[20] Regula Venske, *Das Verschwinden des Mannes in der weiblichen Schreibmaschine. Männerbilder in der Literatur von Frauen* (Hamburg; Zurich, Luchterhand, 1991), 89.

[21] Libuše Moníková, *Eine Schädigung* (first edn. 1981; Munich, dtv, 1990), 27.

[22] See David Harvey, *The Condition of Postmodernity*, 267; and Elizabeth Wilson, *The Sphinx in the City*, 21–3.

[23] 'Jana schaut beängstigt zurück zur Altstadt. Von hier kann sie die Mauern nicht deutlich unterscheiden, sie wirken unverändert, aber wann hat sie sie zum letztenmal ganz aus der Nähe gesehen? Sie möchte sie gleich prüfen, die bröckelnden Stellen zusammenhalten, aber Handauflegen ist zu wenig': Moníková, *Eine Schädigung*, 50.

[24] Ibid., 103.

[25] Ibid., 32. This is reminiscent also of Georg Simmel's 'blasé' attitude of city dwellers, their reserve and concealed aversion to others being both a negative affect of urban life and a survival mechanism: Simmel, 'The metropolis and mental life', 332.

[26] Moníková, *Eine Schädigung*, 33.

[27] Mazzoleni, 'The city and the imaginary', 100.

[28] Moníková, *Eine Schädigung*, 81.

[29] Jana's ambivalence towards the two cultures she inhabits is reflected in her relationships to two men: her lover Jan, whose name and disconcerting vulnerability point to his Czech identity, and her husband Jakob, whose technological practicality and brisk efficiency mark him as German.

[30] Sigrid Weigel, *Die Stimme der Medusa. Schreibweisen in der Gegenwartsliteratur von Frauen* (first edn. 1987; Reinbek, Rowohlt, 1989), 121.

[31] This interpretation is based on the references in the novel to the Argentinian writer Jorge Luis Borges, and on Moníková's critical essays on Borges, which focus on his interest in anthropological and linguistic issues. In particular, one essay concerns Borges's interest in Levi-Strauss's notion of 'productive reduction', the process whereby disability/difference acquire meaning for us in myths. Quoting Levi-Strauss, she writes: 'Blind and lame people, people with one eye or one arm are common mythological figures all over the world, and they confuse us because their condition appears negative to us. But just as a system is rendered discrete by the subtraction of elements, and thereby more logical, if less numerous, thus also the crippled and infirm add positive meaning to myths; they embody modes of mediation': 'Portrait aus mythischen Konnexionen', in Libuše Moníková, *Schloß, Aleph, Wunschtorte. Essays* (Munich; Vienna, Hanser, 1990), 107–18, here 109. Thus I see Francine's voluntary 'disability' as a positive attempt to fix meaning, rather than just a metaphor for alienation.

[32] Libuše Moníková, *Pavane für eine verstorbene Infantin* (first edn. 1983; Munich, dtv, 1988), 74.

[33] Ibid., 26.

[34] Ibid., 79.

[35] In an age when cosmopolitanism has been replaced by multiculturalism and ethnic self-determination on the liberal agenda, there is nothing essentially reactionary about such claims to national liberation and cultural revival. Moreover, as Andreas Huyssens states, contemporary postmodernism 'operates in a field of tension [. . .] which can no longer be grasped in categories such as progress vs. reaction, Left vs. Right, present vs. past, modernism vs. realism, abstraction vs. representation, avantgarde vs. Kitsch. The fact that such dichotomies, which after all are central to the classical accounts of modernism, have broken down is part of the shift I have been trying to describe': Huyssens, 'Mapping the postmodern', 48.

[36] Moníková, *Pavane für eine verstorbene Infantin*, 57 f..

[37] Elizabeth Wilson acknowledges this as a near-universal aspect of village and small-town life: 'There is no evidence that the small community would necessarily be a society freed from surveillance. Indeed, it is much more likely to be more strictly controlled, and would offer none of the opportunities for escape, anonymity, secret pleasures, or even public crowds, that the great city offers': Wilson, *The Sphinx in the City*, 155.

[38] This can be seen illustrated in Irene's habitual gestures: *RB*, 28.

[39] Mazzoleni, 'The city and the imaginary', 95.

[40] For the passage in the novel see *RB*, 133 f..

[41] Mazzoleni, 'The city and the imaginary', 95.

[42] For an account of developments in the cultural interpretation of fashion in the twentieth century, see Katharina Rutschky, 'Unecht, zwecklos, albern. Über Mode als Medium weiblicher Identitätsbildung', *Merkur*, 45 Nos. 9–10 (1991), 812–23.

[43] Mazzoleni, 'The city and the imaginary', 101.

[44] Ibid., 100.

[45] See *TS*, 21; also Interview 'Essen mit Herta Müller', in *Vogue (Deutsch)*, 1 (January 1993), 112 f., here 112.

[46] 'In the lives of emperors there is a moment which follows pride in the boundless extension of the territories we have conquered, and the melancholy and relief of knowing we shall soon give up any thought of knowing and understanding them'. Italo Calvino, *Invisible Cities* (San Diego; New York; London, Harcourt Brace, 1974), 5.

[47] Calvino, *Invisible Cities*, 125; *RB*, 94.

[48] Calvino, *Invisible Cities*, 69.

[49] Braidotti, *Nomadic Subjects*, 24.

[50] Brigid Haines has identified a significant shift in Moníková's writing immediately after the 'Velvet Revolution', detecting in *Treibeis* (1992) a postmodern cultural relativism absent from her earlier novels. In the absence of an obvious oppressor to resist, her political engagement on behalf of the Czechs was noticeably diffused: Haines, 'New places from which to write histories of peoples', 510 f.

6

Metapher, Metonymie und Moral.
Herta Müllers *Herztier*

RICARDA SCHMIDT

Daß, wie Reinhart Koselleck schrieb, »die Wahrheit einer Geschichte [. . .] immer eine Wahrheit *ex post*«[1] ist, erweist sich an
der Themenwahl in Herta Müllers literarischem Werk. 1987 von
Rumänien nach Westberlin übergesiedelt, hat Müller zwar in
Reisende auf einem Bein (1989) ihre Erfahrung von der Ankunft im
Westen literarisch verarbeitet, sich dann aber literarisch nicht
weiter auf die bundesrepublikanische Gegenwart eingelassen, son-
dern sich wieder ihrem Hauptthema zugewandt: der Analyse der
Auswirkungen der – inzwischen überwundenen – rumänischen
Diktatur auf das Alltagsleben besonders im deutschstämmigen
Banat, wo sie ihre Kindheit verbracht hat.

Bereits vor dem Zusammenbruch des Ostblocks unterschieden
sich Müllers literarische Arbeiten aus den frühen 80er Jahren von
denen der meisten regimekritischen Schriftsteller in der DDR
dadurch, daß Müller der Geschichte keinen teleologischen Sinn
unterlegte – auch keinen, der faktisch durch ein Regime mit sozialistischen Prätentionen verhindert wurde, der aber kritischen Intel-
lektuellen als Ideal noch klar vor Augen stand, selbst wenn sie ihn
literarisch primär nur noch *ex negativo* evozieren konnten. Herta
Müllers Arbeiten sind dagegen von einem Kleist noch übertreffen-
den Skeptizismus sowohl der Gesellschaft als auch dem Individuum und dem Geltungsanspruch von Idealen gegenüber getränkt.[2]
Die Erforschung der Diskrepanz zwischen den Intentionen des
Individuums und seinem Handlungsspielraum, seinen Träumen
und seinen Taten, auch der Abgründigkeit menschlicher Verhal-
tensweisen speziell unter den Bedingungen einer Diktatur ist das
Movens in Müllers Werken. In ihnen kommt ästhetisch die ge-
schichtsphilosophische Einsicht zum Ausdruck:

Die Gesamtgeschichte bleibt unvernünftig. Vernünftig ist höchstens
ihre Analyse. Das Absurde, das Aporetische, das Unlösbare, die Unsin-
nigkeiten und Widersinnigkeiten [. . .] lassen sich zwar analytisch auf
einen Begriff bringen, und sie lassen sich auch durch Erzählung in
Anschauung überführen. Wir bedürfen sogar der Erzählung, um das
Aporetische zu veranschaulichen, um es überhaupt einsichtig machen
zu können, auch wenn es nicht rational verständlich oder begreiflich
gemacht werden kann. Was begriffen wird, beruht nur auf der Analyse
ex post. Insofern ergänzen Analyse und Erzählung einander, um unsere
Urteilskraft zu schärfen, um überhaupt mit der Sinnlosigkeit umgehen
zu lernen.[3]

Auch nach dem Sturz der rumänischen Diktatur unterstellt Müller
den geschichtlichen Prozeß nicht einem höheren Sinn oder einem
universalen Ziel, die das Leiden in der Diktatur rechtfertigen
würden, sondern zeigt seine Aporien auf. Obwohl die fiktionale
Darstellung eines in sich abgerundeten sinnvollen Lebens sowie
lineares, geschlossenes Erzählen nie im künstlerischen Horizont
Herta Müllers lagen, erscheint aber bei Müller dennoch die Wirklichkeit gerade nicht, wie Claudia Becker behauptet, »ebenso fragmentarisch wie zusammenhanglos«.[4] Vielmehr geht es Müller
darum, die historisch-politischen Bedingungen sichtbar zu machen, unter denen Wirklichkeit als fragmentarisch und zusammenhanglos erfahren wird. Müller stiftet durch ihre Prosa zwar nicht
Sinn, aber doch Kohärenz zwischen disparaten Elementen, wenn
sie erzählerisch-poetisch die weit- und tiefgehenden Auswirkungen der Diktatur auf das Leben der Individuen zur Anschauung
bringt. Sieht Michael Günther die besondere Eigenart und Qualität
von Müllers Prosa in der »sich eines Urteils enthaltende[n] Kunst
der Beschreibung«,[5] so gehe ich hier vielmehr mit Hayden White
davon aus, daß Erzählen nicht von Moralisieren zu trennen ist
und daß ein Diskurs ein Apparat für die Produktion von Bedeutung ist.[6] Eine zentrale Funktion in Müllers Art zu erzählen
kommt ihren Metaphern und Metonymien zu, in denen sich das
Urteil der Erzählerin über die beschriebene Welt manifestiert.

Seit Aristoteles galt bis in die jüngste Zeit die Metapher als eine
der Erklärung bedürftige Sonderform sprachlichen Ausdrucks, die
von der normalen wörtlich zu verstehenden Sprache abweicht,
indem sie einen Begriff aus einem Bereich auf einen anderen über-
trägt und dabei nach dem Prinzip der Ähnlichkeit verfährt. In der
neueren Metapherntheorie dagegen wird hervorgehoben, daß die
Metapher keineswegs die Ausnahme, sondern vielmehr die Norm

sowohl in der Alltagssprache als auch der Wissenschaftssprache ist.[7] Nach George Lakoff liegt der Ort der Metapher »not in language at all, but in the way we conceptualize one mental domain in terms of another«.[8] Dabei hilft die Metapher uns, »to understand a relatively abstract or inherently unstructured subject matter in terms of a more concrete, or at least highly structured subject matter«.[9] Diese theoretische Einebnung des Unterschieds zwischen wörtlicher und bildlicher Sprache wird einerseits epistemologisch für die Begründung einer konstruktivistischen Position herangezogen, nach der »truly veridical epistemological access to reality is denied [. . . and] cognition is the result of mental *construction*«.[10] Andererseits wird durch diese Einebnung die individuelle poetisch-kreative Konstruktion vernachlässigt zugunsten des Konzepts sozialer Diskurse mit konventionellen Metaphern, die automatisch wie der Rest des linguistischen Systems verwendet werden und »uns sprechen«, d.h. den Menschen zum Produkt der Sprache machen. Daß Müller der Vorwurf gemacht wurde, exzessiv metaphorisch zu schreiben,[11] weist darauf hin, daß zwischen konventionalisierten Metaphern einerseits, deren Bedeutung in sozialen Diskursen so fixiert ist, daß sie zum Teil schon zu lexikalischen Einträgen geworden sind, und poetischen Metaphern andererseits eben doch ein wichtiger Unterschied besteht. Denn eine konventionalisierte Metapher ist das, was Aristoteles »Bezeichnung« nannte, nämlich »ein Nomen, das alle gebrauchen«.[12] Bei poetischen Metaphern dagegen werden zwei mentale Bereiche neu aufeinander bezogen. Hier ist eine Kreativität im Spiel, der eine kognitive Funktion zugesprochen werden kann, und die manchmal in der Lage ist, »new knowledge and insight by *changing* relationships between the things designated«[13] hervorzubringen. LeserInnen, die an die mit konventionalisierten Metaphern gesättigte Alltagssprache gewöhnt sind, kann die Notwendigkeit aktiver Beteiligung an der Sinnherstellung poetischer Metaphern überfordern. Andererseits kann aber auch der Autor/ die Autorin durch Überfrachtung für mangelnde Verständigung verantwortlich sein. Aristoteles schrieb:

Die beste Sprachform ist diejenige, die klar und nicht gewöhnlich ist. Am klarsten ist sie mit den bezeichnenden Nomina, aber dann ist sie gewöhnlich. [. . .] Erhaben und das Gewöhnliche meidend ist die Dichtung, die fremdartige Wörter gebraucht. Fremdartig nenne ich die Glosse, die Metapher, die Erweiterung und alles außerhalb des

Bezeichnenden. Wenn aber einer ausschließlich derartiges in seiner Dichtung anwendet, so wird sie entweder ein Rätsel oder ein Barbarismus [. . .].[14]

Am Beispiel des Romans *Herztier* von 1994 möchte ich hier untersuchen, wie bei Müller Metapher und Metonymie als erzählerische Bindungselemente funktionieren und welche moralisch-politischen Einsichten dadurch nahegelegt werden. Während Metapher und Metonymie z.T. als komplementäre Stilmittel verstanden werden, weil die Metapher auf der Relation der Ähnlichkeit beruht, Metonymie auf dem Prinzip der Kontiguität, geht es mir hier weniger um die Differenz zwischen ihnen, sondern um die Gemeinsamkeit, die ihnen als Tropus eignet. Darin folge ich John R. Searle, für den

it becomes a matter of terminology whether we want to construe metonymy and synecdoche as special cases of metaphor or as independent tropes. When one says, 'S is P,' and means that 'S is R,' P and R may be associated by such relations as the part–whole relation, the container–contained relation, or even the clothing and wearer relation. In each case, as in metaphor proper, the semantic content of the P term conveys the semantic content of the R term by some principle of association.[15]

Die poetische Metapher und Metonymie sind beide semantisch vielfältig, denn sie beziehen verschiedene Bedeutungsbereiche aufeinander, deren Ähnlichkeit oder Kontiguität es für die LeserInnen erst noch zu entdecken gilt – im Gegensatz zur konventionalisierten Metaphorik, die zu semantischer Eindeutigkeit tendiert. Dan Sperber und Deirdre Wilson definieren die Besonderheit poetischer Metaphorik innerhalb eines als Kontinuum verstandenen Systems sprachlicher Kompetenz folgendermaßen:

In general, the wider the range of potential implicatures and the greater the hearer's responsibility for constructing them, the more poetic the effect, the more creative the metaphor. A good creative metaphor is precisely one in which a variety of contextual effects can be retained and understood as weakly implicated by the speaker. In the richest and most successful cases, the hearer or reader can go beyond just exploring the immediate context and the entries for concepts involved in it, accessing a wide area of knowledge, adding metaphors of his own as interpretations of possible developments he is not ready to go into, and getting more and more weak implicatures, with suggestions for still further processing. The result is quite a complex picture, for which the hearer has to take a large part of the responsibility, but the discovery of which has been triggered by the writer. The surprise or beauty of a successful creative metaphor lies in this condensation, in the fact that a single expression which has itself been loosely used will determine a very wide range of acceptable weak implicatures.[16]

Daß aber trotz aller Offenheit der Bedeutungskonstitution poetischer Metaphern diese Offenheit nicht grenzenlos ist, sondern kontextabhängig, betont Richard Boyd, wenn er schreibt:

Literary interaction metaphors, it would seem, display what might be termed *conceptual open-endedness*: they work by inviting the reader (or hearer) to consider the principal subject of the metaphor in the light of associated implications – typically – of the commonplace conception of the secondary subject. Even in those cases in which the metaphor depends upon esoteric information about the secondary subject, the information is of the sort the sufficiently sophisticated reader might be expected to possess (sophisticated commonplaces, so to speak); indeed, the whole point of most literary metaphors would be lost if this sort of knowledge on the part of readers could not be presupposed.[17]

Obwohl literarische Metaphern kontextabhängig sind, können sie durch imaginative Fusionen einen neuen Diskurs über die Wirklichkeit kreieren, denn die Metapher ist, wie Robert Scholes schrieb, »rooted in the naming function of language«.[18] Eine andere Benennung der Wirklichkeit kartographiert also die Wirklichkeit anders, stellt neue Verbindungen her, legt ein anderes Wertsystem nahe.

Im folgenden werde ich mich auf die Metaphorik und Metonymie in der Einleitung von Herta Müllers Roman *Herztier* und einiger im Roman gehäuft auftretender Redewendungen (vor allem: Frisör und Nagelschere, Blechschafe und Holzmelonen, Herztier, Friedhöfe machen, grüne Pflaumen essen) konzentrieren, um an ihnen eine implizite moralische Wertung der dargestellten Realität zu diskutieren. Der Roman erzählt mit vielen Rückblenden in die Kindheit der Erzählerin von verschiedenen freundschaftlichen Beziehungen im Rumänien Ceauşescus, von denen die meisten mit dem Tod enden. Beginnend mit der Erinnerung an die sex- und aufstiegshungrige Lola, von der sich die Erzählerin zu Lebzeiten wegen ihrer Nähe zur Partei ferngehalten hat, wird der destruktive Einfluß des totalitären Regimes auf das Leben verschiedener Individuen erkundet. Erst nachdem sie von der

Bigotterie eines Parteibonzen in den Selbstmord getrieben wurde, rückt Lola der Erzählerin durch ihr Tagebuch nahe, das zum Bindeglied mit den drei Freunden Edgar, Georg und Kurt wird. Doch auch Freundschaft kann nicht verhindern, daß Verzweiflung den einen zum Selbstmord treibt und der andere einen mysteriösen Tod findet. Komplementär zur erst posthum erkannten Nähe zu Lola thematisiert die Beziehung der Erzählerin zu Tereza eine innige Freundschaft zweier Frauen aus unterschiedlichen sozialen Kreisen, die dennoch den Verrat der Freundin an den Geheimdienst mit einschließt. Selbstmord, womöglich Mord, Krebstod, Wahnsinn, Flucht oder Auswanderung werden in *Herztier* als Endstationen des Lebens im totalitären Rumänien dargestellt.

In einer dialogischen Einleitung, nämlich einem Gespräch zwischen der Erzählerin und ihrem Freund Edgar, werden in poetischer Verdichtung Thema und Intention des Romans vorgestellt, nämlich die Aporie des Sprechens über die Opfer einer Diktatur: »Wenn wir schweigen, werden wir unangenehm, sagte Edgar, wenn wir reden, werden wir lächerlich« (*HT*, 7). Der gleiche Satz beendet den Roman, fordert die LeserInnen also auf zu reflektieren, ob und wie es dem Roman gelungen ist, diese Aporie zu umgehen oder zumindest deren Bedingungen einsichtig zu machen. Wenn etwas tun oder es zu unterlassen beide negative Folgen haben, bleibt dem Einzelnen keine Möglichkeit, vernünftig zu handeln. Das Konzept des selbstbestimmten, geschichtsmächtigen Subjekts ist suspendiert. Das Individuum hat nicht die Möglichkeit, richtig zu handeln, aber auch nicht, überhaupt nicht zu handeln.

Noch zwei weitere Male werden in der Einleitung die beiden entgegengesetzten Handlungsweisen reden und schweigen verschmolzen, indem ihnen jeweils gleiche, doch von einander unterschiedene, ja vielleicht sogar sich widersprechende Konsequenzen zugeordnet werden. Zunächst umreißt die Erzählerin die Destruktivität von reden/schweigen mit der Metapher des Zertretens: »Mit den Wörtern im Mund zertreten wir so viel wie mit den Füßen im Gras. Aber auch mit dem Schweigen« (*HT*, 7). Gras scheint hier für einen organischen Zusammenhang zu stehen, der der Gewalt der Rede/des Schweigens von Menschen passiv ausgesetzt ist. Gras und zertreten verhalten sich in dieser Metapher wie Opfer und Akt des Täters zueinander. Im letzten Absatz der Einleitung wird dagegen das Reden/Schweigen mit dem kultivierenden Akt des Grasmähens assoziiert, der aber die Produktivität der

Natur nie endgültig unter Kontrolle halten kann: »Das Gras steht
im Kopf. Wenn wir reden, wird es gemäht. Aber auch, wenn wir
schweigen. Und das zweite, dritte Gras wächst nach, wie es will.
Und dennoch haben wir Glück« (*HT*, 8). Zunächst ist auffällig, daß
Gras hier introjiziert ist, es steht dem handelnden Menschen nicht
als Objekt gegenüber, sondern ist in ihm. Zudem scheint es an
dieser Stelle eher negativ konnotiert zu sein durch den Kontext,
den die vorhergehenden Abstrakta Fehler und Angst bilden. In
seiner Regenerationskraft ist es von den Handlungen des Menschen wenig beeinflußt, ist stärker als er. Der Bedeutungsgehalt
der Metapher Gras oszilliert also ebenso wie die ihm zugeordnete
menschliche Handlung. Wenn entgegengesetzte Handlungen glei-
ches bewirken können, was sowohl Negatives als auch, vorüberge-
hend zumindest, Positives sein kann, wird die Absurdität der Welt
ansichtig. Dem Wort an sich wird keine heilende Kraft zugesprochen, sondern die Möglichkeit seiner destruktiven Wirkung und
einer nur intermittierend eindämmenden Kraft verweist auf die
pragmatische Kontextabhängigkeit des Wortes.

Metonymisch wird in der Assoziationskette der Erzählerin die
Metapher vom »Zertreten mit den Füßen im Gras« verknüpft mit
dem, was in konventionalisierter Semantik unter dem Gras liegt,
dem Grab, sowie mit Gegenständen, die vier verschiedene Todes-
arten evozieren: Gürtel, Fenster, Nuß, Strick. Es sind, so stellt sich
im Verlauf des Romans heraus, mit dem Selbstmord der Kommili-
tonin Lola, des Freundes Georg, dem Krebstod der Freundin
Tereza und dem Tod Kurts assoziierte Objekte. Jeder Tod, so ge-
neralisiert die Erzählerin, ist für sie »wie ein Sack« (*HT*, 7). Ein
Sack verhüllt heterogene Inhalte auf grobe Weise und dient ihrem
unzeremoniellen Transport zur weiteren Verwendung – im impli-
zierten Gegensatz zu der Erhabenheit von Charons Kahn, der Tote
zum dauernden Aufenthalt in den Hades transportierte.

Jeder Tote erscheint der Erzählerin »einen Sack mit Wörtern
hinter sich« (*HT*, 7) zu lassen. Hier scheint hinter der Antinomie
reden/schweigen als dritte Möglichkeit auf, Wörter als Vermächt-
nis derjenigen zum Ausdruck zu bringen, die an der Unvernunft
der Diktatur zugrundegegangen sind. Lolas Tagebuch, Briefe und
erinnerte Gespräche fungieren im Roman als polyphone Erweite-
rungen der Stimme der Erzählerin. Daß die Erzählerin die evozier-
ten Todesfälle ursächlich in Zusammenhang mit der Diktatur
stellen will, wird deutlich, wenn Lebende und Tote nicht nur hinsichtlich der Notwendigkeit, ihren Körper Ordnungssystemen zu

unterwerfen, voneinander unterschieden werden (Tote brauchen keinen Frisör und keine Nagelschere mehr, verlieren nie mehr einen Knopf), sondern vor allem hinsichtlich ihrer Reaktion auf das sie in Rumänien umgebende »Ordnungssystem« einer totalitären Diktatur: »Sie spürten vielleicht anders als wir, daß der Diktator ein Fehler ist, sagte Edgar« (*HT*, 7).

Fehler ist hier ein ontologisches Attribut seines Seins, nicht seines Tuns. Die Personifizierung des Satzsubjektes (Diktator anstelle des zu erwartenden Abstraktums Diktatur) kontrastiert also mit der Totalisierung der Satzaussage und bildet so die politische Struktur der Diktatur auf sprachlicher Ebene mimetisch nach. Der paradoxe Effekt des Diktators, der ein Fehler ist, besteht nun darin, daß im Verhältnis zu ihm nicht etwa alle anderen richtig/fehlerfrei sind, sondern von ihm kontaminiert sind und gerade darin den Beweis des ontologischen Fehlers sehen: »Sie hatten den Beweis, weil auch wir für uns selber ein Fehler waren. Weil wir in diesem Land gehen, essen, schlafen und jemanden lieben mußten in Angst, bis wir wieder den Frisör und die Nagelschere brauchten« (*HT*, 7).

Nun zeigt aber der Roman nur im Falle von Lola innenperspektivisch durch Zitate aus ihrem Tagebuch, daß sie für sich selbst ein Fehler war und benennt den konkreten Anlaß ihres Todes: eine uneheliche Schwangerschaft von einem führenden Parteimitglied, das sie denunziert sowie ihr Wunsch, ihrem Kind Armut und Schande ersparen zu wollen. Georg, der sich nach seiner Ausreise in die Bundesrepublik umbringt, scheint von seinen Erfahrungen in der Diktatur eine so schwere Depression davongetragen zu haben, daß die Hilfe von Freunden und auch das Leben im Westen ihn nicht mehr heilen können. Er wird jedoch vorwiegend von außen dargestellt, so daß die LeserInnen nur aus der metaphorischen Evozierung der Atmosphäre in der totalitären Diktatur und aus der Schilderung seines Verhaltens aus der Sicht der Freunde eine kausale Beziehung für seinen Selbstmord herstellen können. Noch weniger eindeutig ist die Todesursache im Falle von Kurt: Mord oder, wie es offiziell heißt, Selbstmord? Daß Tereza, die Verräterin, auch in der Reihe der Opfer der Diktatur genannt wird, deutet darauf hin, daß ihre Krebserkrankung als Ausdruck psychischer Spannungen gelesen werden kann: zwischen Liebe zur Freundin und dem Druck der Diktatur zerrieben. Die Tatsache, daß der Roman überwiegend eine konkretistische Ursache-Wirkungs-Relation vermeidet, sondern vielmehr Lebensmomente

in einer Diktatur vorführt, ist als konstruktive Antwort auf die
zitierte Aporie des Redens oder Schweigens über die Opfer der
Diktatur zu lesen: weder durch Schweigen zum Unrecht des Regimes beitragen, noch durch Reden zu vereinfachen.
Fungierten Frisör und Nagelschere zunächst als Unterschei-
dungsmerkmale zwischen Lebenden und Toten, so steht ihr
regelmäßig wiederkehrender Bedarf im oben zitierten Satz im
Gegensatz zu anderen menschlichen Grundbedürfnissen, die im
Zustand der Angst befriedigt werden müssen. Welche menschlichen Bedürfnisse und Erfahrungen mit der metonymisch durch
die Worte Frisör und Nagelschere bezeichneten Regulierung der
stets wachsenden Körperauswüchse assoziiert werden, erhellt sich
erst im Verlauf des Romans. Für die aus einer armgebliebenen
Gegend kommende Studentin Lola, die vor ihrem Selbstmord ihr
Tagebuch der Erzählerin in den Koffer steckt, ist der Hausbesuch
des Frisörs ein erträumtes, doch nie erreichtes Statussymbol (vgl.
HT, 11, 13). Als Kind hört die Erzählerin den Frisör des Groß-
vaters sagen: »Wenn man die Haare nicht schneidet, wird der
Kopf ein Gestrüpp« (*HT*, 17). Kopf mag sich hier sowohl auf das
Äußere als auch das Innere, d.h. die Gedanken, beziehen. Der
Frisör etabliert sich gegenüber dem Kind als Statthalter einer
geradezu metaphysischen Ordnungsmacht, zumal das Kind diesen
Satz hört, während es von der Mutter mit Gürteln an einen Stuhl
gebunden wird, weil es sich nicht die Nägel schneiden lassen will.
»Der Frisör sagt: Wenn man die Nägel nicht schneidet, werden die
Finger zu Schaufeln. Nur die Toten dürfen sie tragen« (*HT*, 17).
Das Kind jedoch phantasiert Nägelschneiden als Fingerabschneid-
en (vgl. *HT*, 14 f.) und die Mutter als fingeressende
Exekutionsmacht, der es wehrlos ausgeliefert ist. Beim gewaltsam-
en Nägelschneiden des Kindes tropft Blut auf »einen der Gürtel,
auf den grasgrünen [. . .] Das Kind weiß: Wenn man blutet, dann
stirbt man« (*HT*, 14). Später erhängt sich Lola am Gürtel der Erzählerin (vgl. *HT*, 30) und bei der Spurensicherung verwendet die
Polizei »giftgrünen Staub« (*HT*, 30). So werden Nägelschneiden,
Gürtel und die Farbe grün mit der gesellschaftlichen Platzanwei-
sung an das Individuum assoziiert. Doch bezahlt das Individuum
in einer totalitären Gesellschaft diesen Platz mit einer Beschnei-
dung seines Lebens durch brutale Ordnungsmächte auf familiärer
und staatlicher Ebene, die sich über die Bedürfnisse des Individuums hinwegsetzen. Daß später die Freunde für ihre Briefe einen
Code verabreden, in dem »Ein Satz mit Nagelschere für Verhör«

(*HT*, 90) steht, bestätigt den repressiven Charakter der mit der Nagelschere konnotierten Ordnung. Einzig Lola scheint zeitweilig einen Weg gefunden zu haben, eine »Ordnung der Nägel« (d.h. der unwillkürlich wachsenden Körperauswüchse) ohne Fesselung zu verwirklichen. Ihre Art, sich die Nägel immer in der Straßenbahn mit einer von der Mitschülerin ausgeliehenen Schere zu schneiden (vgl. *HT*, 18), kommt als vagabundierende Ordnung vielleicht dem Wunsch des zum Nägelschneiden gefesselten Kindes nach »Losbinden, losbinden« (*HT*, 17) nahe.

Der Frisör steht ebenso wie das Nägelschneiden für Deformationen, die das Leben im Totalitarismus in scheinbar ganz persönlichen, unpolitischen Bereichen prägen. Denn jegliche Form von Individualität wird unterdrückt, und so wird der Frisör Teil der exekutiven Gewalt der Diktatur. Nachdem die Freunde als kritische Geister dem staatlichen Überwachungsapparat ins Visier kommen, träumt Kurt wiederholt, daß seine Außenseiterposition ihm durch den die Norm vertretenden Frisör vermittelt wird. Ihm träumt, daß sein Frisör ihn nicht kennt und daß er ihm die Haare nicht schneiden will, weil er Schamhaare im Gesicht hat (vgl. *HT*, 78 f.): d.h. das Private wird bei ihm öffentlich, und er schämt sich dafür. Als die Überwachungsorgane zur Einschüchterung der oppositionellen Jungen deren Rasiermesser aus ihren verschlossenen Koffern verschwinden lassen, träumt Kurt, daß beim Frisör die Kunden Kreuzworträtsel lösen müssen, bevor sie eine Frisur bekommen und daß der Frisör gerade das ihm Fehlende verlangt: »Bringen Sie morgen Ihr Messer von zu Hause mit.« (*HT*, 85). Es ist der Frisör, der die Reihenfolge bestimmt, in der er seinen Kunden die Haare schneidet (vgl. *HT*, 86) und der die Haare eines Kunden stellvertretend für alle die anderen schert, die lange nicht kommen (vgl. *HT*, 228).

In solchen Bildern des scheinbar unpolitischen Privatlebens und des Träumens fängt Herta Müller das absurde Wesen des Totalitarismus noch eindrücklicher ein als in den Berichten von Verhören durch Hauptmann Pjele und seinen gleichnamigen Hund. Ebenso wie Herr und Hund austauschbar werden, werden die Arbeiter zu bloßen Funktionen ihres Berufszweigs. Da es wegen der bekanntlich schlechten Versorgungslage in den sozialistischen Ländern für nicht privilegierte Arbeiter nicht viel zu kaufen gab, stehlen sie das ihnen Zugängliche am Arbeitsplatz und überziehen ihre ganze Wohnung damit. Der Totalitarismus mit seiner Tendenz zur Uniformität konkretisiert sich als Szenerie eines absurden

Theaterstücks, wenn beim Arbeiter aus der Pelzbranche Sofakissen, Bettdecken, Stuhlpolster, Teppiche, Hausschuhe, selbst Topflappen aus Pelz sind (vgl. *HT*, 191); wenn die Arbeiter der holzverarbeitenden Industrie Parkett nicht nur auf allen Fußböden ihrer Wohnungen, sondern auch die Wände hoch verlegen; wenn die Arbeiter aus dem Schlachthaus die Kleinigkeiten geschlachteter Tiere stehlen, Kuhschwänze als Flaschenbürsten und Kinderspielzeug nach Hause bringen und süchtig das frische Blut der Tiere saufen. Selbst ein Kind, das Fahrkartenkontrolleur mit sich selbst spielt, hat bereits das Prinzip des Totalitarismus verinnerlicht und lehnt das Angebot eines Nachbarn zum Mitspielen ab: »Ich bin lieber alles zusammen, sagte das Kind, dann weiß ich, wer seine Karte nicht findet« (*HT*, 194).

Ausgehend von Lolas Tagebuchsatz über ihre Erfahrung in der arm gebliebenen Gegend, daß die Dürre alles frißt »außer den Schafen, Melonen und Maulbeerbäumen« (*HT*, 9), setzt der Roman Schafe und Melonen als Metaphern für Armut, Mangel, vergebliche Arbeit ein und Maulbeerbäume als Metapher für Träume von einem besseren Leben, die man aus der armen Gegend mitnimmt und die das Gesicht zeichnen: »In Lolas Heft las ich später: Was man aus der Gegend hinausträgt, trägt man hinein in sein Gesicht« (*HT*, 10). Alte Leute haben Maulbeerbäume vom Land in die Innenhöfe der Stadt getragen und sitzen nun einsam in ihrem Schatten. Lolas Männer waren Bauern, die ihre Dörfer verlassen haben, um in Fabriken zu arbeiten: »Nie wieder Schafe, hatten auch sie gesagt, nie wieder Melonen« (*HT*, 36). Diese Hoffnung entlarvt die Erzählerin als Illusion: »Die Männer wußten, daß ihr Eisen, ihr Holz, ihr Waschpulver nichts zählten. Deshalb blieben ihre Hände klobig, sie machten Klötze und Klumpen statt Industrie. Alles, was groß und eckig sein sollte, wurde in ihren Händen ein Schaf aus Blech. Was klein und rund sein sollte, wurde in ihren Händen eine Melone aus Holz« (*HT*, 37).

Hier wird in einem Zirkelschluß das Wissen der Männer um die Wertlosigkeit ihrer Produktion als die Ursache ihrer Ungeschicklichkeit bei der Arbeit und der mechanischen Reproduktion dessen, was sie fliehen wollten, bezeichnet. Dieses Wissen scheint sich hier nicht auf die Produktionsbedingungen im diktatorisch-sozialistischen Rumänien zu beziehen, sondern prinzipiell auf die Unzufriedenheit von Bauern mit industrieller Arbeit. Wenn die Erzählerin vom »Proletariat der Blechschafe und Holzmelonen« (*HT*, 37, 51, 209) spricht; wenn sie Arbeiter Blechschafe halten oder tragen sieht (vgl. *HT*, 140, 179); wenn sie über die Industriestadt, in die Edgar nach dem Studium geschickt wird, sagt: »Alle in dieser Stadt machten Blechschafe und nannten sie Metallurgie« (*HT*, 93); und von Georg berichtet, daß er als Lehrer in eine Industriestadt zugeteilt war, »in der alle Holzmelonen machten. Die Holzmelonen hießen holzverarbeitende Industrie« (*HT*, 97), dann ebnet sie die Unterschiede zwischen verschiedenen Industriezweigen in einer universalisierenden, degradierenden, komischen Neubenennung ein. In den letzten beiden Zitaten wird durch die Satzstruktur des Bildes (das Verb »machen« mit direktem Objekt) der Anschein von faktischer Beschreibung erweckt im Gegensatz zu dem, was in der konventionellen Bezeichnung nur so genannt oder geheißen wird. Die übliche Rechtfertigung von Industrialisierung als Fortschritt wird ironisch konterkariert durch die Wahl von Komposita aus Metaphern und Metonymen, die Dummheit (dummes Schaf, Holzkopf) und mechanisches Spielzeug assoziieren. Daß nun statt echter Schafe und Melonen solche aus Blech und Holz produziert werden, erweckt den Eindruck, das ganze Land sei eine arm gebliebene Gegend – in ihrer billigen Mechanik noch ärmer als die bäuerliche, aus der Lola stammt. Zwar macht diese Metaphorik auf komisch-ironische Weise das Scheitern der Industrialisierung in Rumänien einsichtig, doch beruht der komische Effekt auf der gleichen homogenisierenden, universalisierenden Geste, die der Roman an anderen Stellen als totalitaristisch charakterisiert. Der Eindruck, daß hier Komik auf Kosten von Komplexität, Differenziertheit, Widersprüchlichkeit erzeugt wird, wird noch verstärkt dadurch, daß es nur einen Grund für dieses Scheitern zu geben scheint: die mangelnde Überzeugung der ehemaligen Bauern vom Wert industrieller Arbeit.

Wenn dagegen vom ironisch-komischen Wahrheitsanspruch der Schritt zur Darstellung von Wahnsinn getan wird, scheint im Wahnsinn versteckter Sinn auf, so etwa, wenn von einem verrückten Philosophen berichtet wird, er »verwechselte die Telefonmasten und Baumstämme mit Menschen. Er erzählte dem Eisen und Holz von Kant und dem Kosmos der fressenden Schafe« (*HT*, 48).

Während die Erzählerin durch Metaphern und Metonymie unterschiedliche industrielle Produktionszweige homogenisiert, der agrarischen Produktion des Landes angleicht und so auf das gemeinsame Merkmal der trotz Arbeit nicht überwundenen Armseligkeit reduziert, konstituiert sie, ebenfalls durch sprachliche Stilmittel, eine Kontiguität – wenn auch keine kausal bedingte

Zwangsläufigkeit – von historisch repressiven Regimen: Die Metapher »Friedhöfe machen« bezeichnet sowohl die Tätigkeit des sozialistischen Diktators (vgl. *HT*, 8) als auch des Vaters als SS-Soldat (vgl. *HT*, 21).

Von besonderem Interesse sind überdies Wahrnehmungen, die in der individuellen nationalsozialistischen Familiengeschichte der Erzählerin wurzeln, aber im politischen Kontext der sozialistischen Diktatur neue Resonanz gewinnen. Dazu gehören die metaphorische Aufladung des Essens von grünen Pflaumen und der Begriff Herztier. Als Kind wird die Erzählerin von ihrem Vater mit SS-Vergangenheit vor dem Essen grüner Pflaumen gewarnt (vgl. *HT*, 22). Da aber nach dem Empfinden des Kindes der Vater »dem Kind den Tod wünscht« (*HT*, 22), wendet es die Aggressivität des Vaters gegen sich selbst und ißt heimlich grüne Pflaumen, von denen es gehört hat, daß sie Fieber und Tod verursachen. Grüne Pflaumen werden so mit unbeherrschbaren destruktiven und selbstdestruktiven Tendenzen assoziiert, die ein diktatorisches Regime im Individuum produziert: »Ein Kind hat Angst vor dem Sterben und ißt noch mehr grüne Pflaumen und weiß nicht warum« (*HT*, 90). Daß auch die Wächter in Ceauşescus Diktatur wie besessen grüne Pflaumen essen (vgl. *HT*, 58 ff., 82), macht aus einer Idiosynkrasie ein politisches Symptom, das die Effekte von verschiedenen totalitären Systemen engführt, selbst wenn die individuelle Genese der Bedeutung, die dieser metaphorisch aufgeladenen Tätigkeit beigemessen wird, explizit reflektiert wird: »Auch Edgar, Kurt und Georg aßen als Kinder grüne Pflaumen. Ihnen war kein Pflaumenbild im Kopf geblieben, weil kein Vater sie beim Essen störte. Sie lachten mich aus, wenn ich sagte: Man stirbt und niemand kann helfen, vom hellen Fieber brennt dir von innen das Herz aus« (*HT*, 60 f.). In der rumänischen Sprache jedoch findet die Erzählerin Nahrung für ihre Assoziationen: »Pflaumenfresser war ein Schimpfwort. Emporkömmlinge, Selbstverleugner, aus dem Nichts gekrochene Gewissenlose und über Leichen gehende Gestalten nannte man so. Auch den Diktator nannte man Pflaumenfresser« (*HT*, 59).

Ebenfalls aus der Kindheit der Erzählerin kommt die titelgebende Metapher des Romans, Herztier. Als sie das Kind in den Schlaf sang, sagte die Großmutter zur Erzählerin: »Ruh dein Herztier aus, du hast heute so viel gespielt« (*HT*, 40). Für Josef Zierden wird das »Herztier« der Großmutter »in dieser unwirtlichen Welt für Momente zur Chiffre für Wärme und Vertrauen«.[19] Auch

Walter Hinck sieht es als »den Begriff eines sehr naiven und zärt-
lichen Denkens«.[20] Eine solche positiv-sentimentale Deutung
vernachlässigt jedoch viel von dem Kontext, in dem der Begriff
verwendet wird. Die singende Großmutter ist nämlich, entgegen
dem ersten Eindruck von ihr, für die Erzählerin nicht mit Helle,
sondern mit Dunkelheit assoziiert. Denn sie hat ihr Wissen um
das Herztier im Menschen, d.h. seine Vitalität, seine treibende
Lebenskraft, für eigensüchtige Zwecke eingesetzt:

> Sie weiß, daß jeder ein Herztier hat. Sie nimmt einer anderen Frau den
> Mann weg. Dieser Mann liebt die andere Frau, die singende Großmut-
> ter liebt er nicht. Aber sie bekommt ihn, weil sie ihn haben will. Nicht
> ihn, sondern sein Feld. Und sie behält ihn. Er liebt sie nicht, aber sie
> kann ihn beherrschen, indem sie zu ihm sagt: Dein Herztier ist eine
> Maus.
> Dann war alles umsonst, weil das Feld nach dem Krieg vom Staat
> enteignet wird.
> Vor diesem Entsetzen fing die Großmutter zu singen an. (*HT*, 81)

Daß nach dem Tod des Vaters der Erzählerin, der als SS-Mann
und übelwollender Vater ausschließlich in einem negativen Licht
ohne den kleinsten liebenswerten Zug erscheint, sein Herztier in
der singenden Großmutter hauste (vgl. *HT*, 75), verstärkt zum
einen die Nähe der singenden Großmutter zum Bösen. Zum anderen wird deutlich, daß der treibenden Lebenskraft, die mit dem
Begriff Herztier assoziiert ist, nicht an sich eine moralisch positive
Qualität eignet.

Die Möglichkeit einer bösen treibenden Kraft wird am deutlich-
sten in einer von der Erzählerin imaginierten Szene. Nach Lolas
Tod liegen im Kühlschrank des Studentenwohnheims keine Zungen und Nieren mehr, wie Lola sie von ihren »Freiern« geschenkt
bekam, doch sind sie der Erzählerin trotzdem sinnlich gegenwär-
tig:

> Aber ich sah und roch sie. Ich stellte mir vor dem offenen Kühlschrank
> einen durchsichtigen Mann vor. Der Durchsichtige war krank und
> hatte, um länger zu leben, die Eingeweide gesunder Tiere gestohlen.
> Ich sah sein Herztier. Es hing eingeschlossen in der Glühbirne. Es
> war gekrümmt und müde. Ich schlug den Kühlschrank zu, weil das
> Herztier nicht gestohlen war. Es konnte nur sein eigenes sein, es war
> häßlicher als die Eingeweide aller Tiere dieser Welt. (*HT*, 70)

Da diesem Erzählabschnitt der Bericht von Gerüchten über Krankheiten und grausige Heilmittel des Diktators direkt vorausgeht (»Kinderblut gegen Blutkrebs« *HT*, 70), liegt es nahe, daß hier das häßliche Herztier des Durchsichtigen auf die vitale, doch widerliche Lebenskraft des Diktators anspielt. Demgegenüber empfinden die gegen ihn opponierenden jungen Leute ihre Lebenskraft als schwach und flüchtig:

> Aus jedem Mund kroch der Atem in die kalte Luft. Vor unseren Gesichtern zog ein Rudel fliehender Tiere. Ich sagte zu Georg: Schau, dein Herztier zieht aus. [. . .]
> Unsere Herztiere flohen wie Mäuse. Sie warfen das Fell hinter sich ab und verschwanden im Nichts. Wenn wir kurz nacheinander viel redeten, blieben sie länger in der Luft. (*HT*, 89 f.)

Immerhin jedoch ist das Herztier der Erzählerin stark genug, sie von ihren Selbstmordgedanken abzubringen: »Der Tod pfiff mir von weitem, ich mußte Anlauf nehmen zu ihm. Ich hatte mich fast in der Hand, nur ein winziges Teil machte nicht mit. Vielleicht war es das Herztier« (*HT*, 111). Die titelgebende Metapher des Romans evoziert also eine Lebenskraft von unterschiedlicher Stärke und unterschiedlicher Qualität. Sie kann für die verschiedensten guten und bösen Zwecke eingesetzt werden, und sie ist nicht immun gegen Manipulation, Bedrohung, Einschüchterung, Gewalt. Die Metapher »Herztier« bleibt also tatsächlich, wie Philipp Müller schrieb, »als zentrales Bild des Romans in seiner Rätselgestalt vieldeutig«.[21] Doch Philipp Müllers Identifikation dieser Metapher als »›die Sehnsucht nach Neuem‹, die als ein utopisches Moment nur leere *Form*, nicht gefüllte *Gestalt* des Neuen werden darf«[22] biegt die konstatierte Vieldeutigkeit in eine positive – wenn auch abstrakt bleibende – Sinnsetzung zurück, der der Roman widerstrebt.

Herta Müllers nuancenreiche Bildersprache erzeugt durch ihre Originalität und gerade in der Konzentration auf Details des privaten Alltagslebens eine nachdrückliche Bloßstellung der Diktatur und ihrer enthumanisierenden Wirkung auf den Einzelnen. Diese moralische Position der Erzählerin artikuliert sich in der Auswahl und Variation metaphorischer Beschreibungen, nicht in einem bewertenden Kommentar zu einer angeblich objektiv dargestellten Wirklichkeit. Müllers Interesse gilt primär der Rechtfertigung des Partikularen, das sich dem Anspruch auf universale Gültigkeit und universale Lösungen widersetzt. In dieser Privilegierung des

Besonderen und in der Betonung der möglichen Gleichzeitigkeit
von Freundschaft und Verrat oder Freundschaft und existentieller
Einsamkeit ist Müller durchaus Moralistin ohne universalistische
Moralvorstellungen. Dennoch kann es vorkommen, daß Müller in
ihrem Ziel, Uniformität zu denunzieren, selbst in die Geste homo-
genisierender Metaphorik verfällt, d.h. für die Kritik einer verhaß-
ten Realität die Denkmuster eben dieser Realität benutzt: Der SS-
Vater machte Friedhöfe, sonst nichts. Alle Arbeiter machen
Blechschafe und Holzmelonen, weil sie nicht an den Wert ihrer
Arbeit glauben.

Daß Müllers Medium der kritischen Geschichtsbetrachtung, die
Metapher, auf künstlerischem Gebiet einen Willen zur Macht
signifiziert, wie ihn Sarah Kofman als Charakteristikum der Metaphorik bei Nietzsche herausgearbeitet hat,[23] wird gerade an solchen Fällen in seiner Ambivalenz deutlich. Vielleicht sind solche
problematischen Fälle noch interessanter als die gelungene Neu-
perspektivierung der Realität, zeigen sie doch, wie widersprüch-
lich und komplex unser Denken ist, wie unbewußt in uns das
weiterwirkt, was wir ablehnen und wie schwer es ist, ohne homo-
genisierende Kategorien auszukommen. Auch eine kritische Art
der Historie im Sinne Nietzsches, wie Herta Müller sie betreibt, ist
ja nicht frei von Verzerrungen. Nietzsche schrieb über die kritische
Art, die Vergangenheit zu betrachten:

> Es ist nicht die Gerechtigkeit, die hier zu Gericht sitzt; es ist noch we-
> niger die Gnade, die hier das Urtheil verkündet: sondern das Leben
> allein, jene dunkle, treibende, unersättlich sich selbst begehrende
> Macht. Sein Spruch ist immer ungnädig, immer ungerecht, weil er nie
> aus einem reinen Borne der Erkenntnis geflossen ist [. . .]. Es ist im-
> mer ein gefährlicher, nämlich für das Leben selbst gefährlicher Prozeß:
> und Menschen oder Zeiten, die auf diese Weise dem Leben dienen,
> dass sie eine Vergangenheit richten und vernichten, sind immer
> gefährliche und gefährdete Menschen und Zeiten. Denn da wir nun
> einmal die Resultate früherer Geschlechter sind, sind wir auch die
> Resultate ihrer Verirrungen, Leidenschaften und Irrthümer, ja Verbre-
> chen; es ist nicht möglich sich ganz von dieser Kette zu lösen. Wenn
> wir jene Verirrungen verurtheilen und uns ihrer für enthoben erachten,
> so ist die Thatsache nicht beseitigt, dass wir aus ihnen herstammen.
> Wir bringen es im besten Falle zu einem Widerstreite der ererbten,
> angestammten Natur und unserer Erkenntniss [. . .].[24]

Anmerkungen

[1] Reinhart Koselleck, 'Vom Sinn und Unsinn der Geschichte', *Merkur,* 51 Nr. 4 (April 1997), 319–34, hier 326.

[2] Vgl. auch Herta Müllers Selbsteinschätzung als historisch jenseits selbst des kleinen Kleistschen Hoffnungsfunkens stehend in ihrer Rede anläßlich der Verleihung des Kleist-Preises 1994: »Wo sich bei Kleist ›wenn die Erkenntnis gleichsam durch ein Unendliches gegangen ist, die Grazie wieder einfindet‹, da gelangte die Welt nach dem Nationalsozialismus und nach dem Stalinismus nie mehr hin. Ich hätte auf die Suche nach dieser Unschuld gehen können, aber sie hätte nichts genützt. Denn gezeugt worden war ich nach dem Zweiten Weltkrieg von einem heimgekehrten SS-Soldaten. Und hineingeboren worden war ich in den Stalinismus. Der Vater und die Zeit – beides Tatsachen, die das Sich-wieder-Einfinden der Grazie unwiederbringlich machen« (*HS*, 7–15, hier 9 f.). Vgl. auch Müllers Äußerungen zur Utopie im Gespräch mit Brigid Haines und Margaret Littler: »Diese in die Realität umgesetzten Utopien sind immer ein Unglück geworden. Sie haben immer eine Diktatur ergeben. Für mich ist das völlig logisch. Wenn eine Idee über alles Bescheid weiß, kann sie ja nichts anderes tun, als den Einzelnen nötigen und zwingen«: Vgl. in diesem Band, 22.

[3] Koselleck, 'Vom Sinn und Unsinn der Geschichte', 323 f.

[4] Claudia Becker, '"Serapionisches Prinzip" in politischer Manier. Wirklichkeits- und Sprachbilder in *Niederungen*', in Norbert Otto Eke (Hrsg.) *Die erfundene Wahrnehmung. Annäherung an Herta Müller* (Paderborn, Igel Verlag, 1991) 32–41, hier 36.

[5] Michael Günther, 'Froschperspektiven. Über Eigenart und Wirkung erzählter Erinnerung in Herta Müllers *Niederungen*', in Eke (Hrsg.), *Die erfundene Wahrnehmung,* 42–59, hier 58.

[6] Vgl. Hayden White, *The Content of Form: Narrative Discourse and Historical Representation* (Baltimore; London, The Johns Hopkins University Press, 1992), 25, 42: »Could we ever narrativize without moralizing? [. . .] a discourse is regarded as an apparatus for the production of meaning rather than as only a vehicle for the transmission of information about an extrinsic referent«.

[7] Zur Metapher in der Alltagssprache vgl. George Lakoff, 'The contemporary theory of metaphor', in Andrew Ortony (Hrsg.), *Metaphor and Thought,* 2nd edn. (Cambridge, Cambridge University Press, 1995), 202–51. Zur Metapher in der wissenschaftlichen Theoriebildung vgl. Richard Boyd, 'Metaphor and theory change: what is "metaphor" a metaphor for?', in Ortony (Hrsg.), *Metaphor and Thought*, 481–532.

[8] Lakoff, 'The contemporary theory of metaphor', 203.

[9] Ebd., 245.

[10] Andrew Ortony, 'Metaphor, language and thought', in Ortony (Hrsg.), *Metaphor and Thought*, 1–16, hier 1.

[11] Josef Zierden referiert die Kritik an Müller, mit der »metaphernüberhäuften Poetisierung der Wirklichkeit Gefahr zu laufen, in künstlicher Manier zu erstarren«: 'Herta Müller': *KLG*, 50. Nlg. (1.4.1995), 4,.

[12] Aristoteles, *Poetik*, übersetzt von Olof Gigon (Stuttgart, Reclam, 1961), 54.

[13] Max Black, 'More about metaphor', in Ortony (Hrsg.), *Metaphor and Thought*, 19–41, hier 35.

[14] Aristoteles, *Poetik*, 56.

[15] John R. Searle, 'Metaphor', in Ortony (Hrsg.), *Metaphor and Thought*, 83–111, hier 107.

[16] Dan Sperber und Deirdre Wilson, *Relevance: Communication and Cognition* (Oxford, Blackwell, 1986), 236 f.

[17] Richard Boyd, 'Metaphor and theory change', in Ortony (Hrsg.), *Metaphor and Thought*, 481–532, hier 488.

[18] Robert Scholes, *Semiotics and Interpretation* (New Haven, Yale University Press, 1982), 76.

[19] Zierden, 'Herta Müller', 8.

[20] Walter Hinck, 'Das mitgebrachte Land. Rede zur Verleihung des Kleist-Preises 1994 an Herta Müller', *Kleist-Jahrbuch* (1995), 6–13, hier 7 f.

[21] Philipp Müller, 'Herztier. Ein Titel/Bild inmitten von Bildern', in Ralph Köhnen (Hrsg.), *Der Druck der Erfahrung treibt die Sprache in die Dichtung. Bildlichkeit in Texten Herta Müllers* (Frankfurt am Main, Lang, 1997), 109-121, hier 116.

[22] Ebd.

[23] Vgl. Sarah Kofman, *Nietzsche and Metaphor*, translated by Duncan Large (London, The Athlone Press, 1993), 82.

[24] Friedrich Nietzsche, *Unzeitgemässe Betrachtungen. Zweites Stück: Vom Nutzen und Nachtheil der Historie für das Leben*, in Giorgio Colli und Mazzino Montinari (Hrsg.), *Nietzsche. Werke. Kritische Gesamtausgabe*, 3. Abteilung, 1. Bd. (Berlin; New York, de Gruyter, 1972), 239-330, hier 265 f.

7

'Die Einzelheiten und das Ganze': Herta Müller and Totalitarianism

JOHN J. WHITE

Ich versuche mich immer an den Rand des Geschehens zu denken, das ich wahrnehme. Ich sehe die Menschen, wie sie angeblich frei handeln und dabei nicht wissen, daß sie es unter bestimmten Zwängen tun, daß sie in einem Mechanismus drin stecken, daß sie mit der Freiheit von Marionetten handeln. Ich versuche dann, diesen Mechanismus darzustellen.[1]

The 'mechanisms' which control most behaviour in Herta Müller's novels and stories are on the whole driven by totalitarianism, although the extent to which she successfully lays bare their workings is open to question. Her ongoing series of 'Dramatische Bilder aus Rumäniens Schreckensherrschaft', i.e. under the despotic Ceauşescu-led regime – and her various explorations of the way it could mark its victims, long after they had left their homeland or the ghosts of that particular phase of its history had been laid to rest – comes across, perhaps the artifice implied by her phrase 'sich an den Rand [. . .] denken' already suggests this, as tending towards the idiosyncratic. This is not only because of the surreal quality of many of her early writings, their deliberate combination of estranging focalizer and grotesque imagery (one critic talks of her 'Versuch einer Aneignung der Wirklichkeit durch das gemachte Bild');[2] it also results from a selective concentration on minutiae whose significance is often more implied than explicitly commented on. The ugly larger political realities of daily life under Ceauşescu chronicled in such works as *Niederungen*, *Barfüßiger Februar* and *Der Fuchs war damals schon der Jäger* have, since the events of 1989, become so well-documented that Müller's fiction can nowadays rely on a more informed sense of political

context than would have been available to most of her non-
Romanian readers at the time of first publication. (As Richard
Wagner once put it, 'Was bisher zwischen den Zeilen stand, war
nun im Fernsehen'.)[3] Yet the Romanian 'Wende' has in this respect
not brought about a radical change in Müller's writing: one of the
striking features of even later works like *Herztier* and *Heute wär ich
mir lieber nicht begegnet* remains the extent to which the sheer bar-
barism and regional peculiarities of modern Romanian totalitarianism are presented obliquely, as something to be read 'zwischen
den Zeilen', almost as if too overt a thematization might risk playing totalitarianism's game of politicizing all domains of human
experience, including literature itself. Consequently, Müller's literary works are in many respects more palimpsests of the political
than overtly mimetic reflections of the totalitarian world in which
she grew up.

One exception, the historically explicit anecdote 'Überall, wo
man den Tod gesehen hat' from near the end of *Barfüßiger Februar*,
stands out in marked contrast to the majority of stories around it.
This record of what the subtitle disingenuously refers to as 'Eine
Sommerreise in die Maramuresch' acquires its exceptional status
from its meticulous registering of observed facts: details relating to
the narrator's visit to the Jewish cemetery in Oberwischau, statis-
tics concerning local wartime atrocities, quotations from eyewit-
ness accounts of the period and references to Himmler's two visits
to the region. The extent to which this differs from the fantastic
realism of adjacent stories doubtless has something to do with the
fact that the piece addresses the enormity of what happened in
this location during the early 1940s, not the oppression taking
place at the time of its writing.

In general, however, despite one or two notable exceptions,
Müller's following remark about what attracts her to other dissident writers' work is equally applicable to her own writings: 'Das,
was mich einkreist [. . .] beim Lesen, ist das, was zwischen den
Sätzen fällt und aufschlägt, oder kein Geräusch macht. Es ist das
Ausgelassene' (*TS*, 19). Because the works' effect depends on an
amalgam of what is made explicit and what is left unsaid, and
although the remark does not apply only to the political dimension, the reader is expected to bring considerable background
knowledge to bear on Müller's fictions. As she says in respect of
Barfüßiger Februar: 'Es sind [. . .] sehr viele Erfahrungen – All-
tagserfahrungen – nötig, um zu wissen, was [. . .] gemeint ist. Es

'ist nichts abstrakt in diesem Buch. Nur: ein Leser hier [i.e. in the West] hat nicht den nötigen Hintergrund, um das alles zu wissen'.[4] Of course, one rejoinder would be that with *Der Teufel sitzt im Spiegel, Hunger und Seide* and *In der Falle*, as well as her numerous published interviews and newspaper articles, Müller has over the years done much to foster the requisite sense of political context. Yet when it comes to the treatment of totalitarianism (or, more accurately: 'totalitarianisms' in the plural), she has nevertheless been distinctly selective in what she has singled out for explicit comment and in the way she has chosen to approach her material.

The following two-part excerpt from the beginning of *Herztier* gives some indication of the kind of issues that come into play as 'das Ausgelassene', in a political sense, is hinted at by various strategies of understatement and indirection:

Seit Monaten wechselte Lola einmal in der Woche die Wandzeitung im Glaskasten des Studentenheims. Sie stand neben der Eingangstür und bewegte die Hüften im Glaskasten. Sie blies die toten Fliegen heraus und putzte das Glas mit zwei Patentstrümpfen aus ihrem Koffer. Mit dem einen Strumpf machte sie das Glas naß, mit dem anderen rieb sie es trocken. Dann wechselte sie die Zeitungsausschnitte, zerknäulte die vorletzte Rede des Diktators und klebte die letzte Rede hinein. Wenn Lola fertig war, warf sie die Strümpfe weg.

Als Lola fast alle Patentstrümpfe aus ihrem Koffer für den Glaskasten benutzt hatte, nahm sie die Strümpfe aus den anderen Koffern. Jemand sagte, das sind nicht deine Strümpfe. Lola sagte, die zieht ihr ja doch nicht mehr an.

Ein Vater hackt den Sommer im Garten. Ein Kind steht neben dem Beet und denkt sich: Der Vater weiß was vom Leben. Denn der Vater steckt sein schlechtes Gewissen in die dümmsten Pflanzen und hackt sie ab. Kurz davor hat das Kind sich gewünscht, daß die dümmsten Pflanzen vor der Hacke fliehen und den Sommer überleben. Doch sie können nicht fliehen, weil sie erst im Herbst weiße Federn bekommen. Erst dann lernen sie fliegen.

Der Vater mußte nie fliehen. Er war singend in die Welt marschiert. Er hatte in der Welt Friedhöfe gemacht und die Orte schnell verlassen. Ein verlorener Krieg, ein heimgekehrter SS-Soldat, ein frischgebügeltes Sommerhemd lag im Schrank, und auf dem Kopf des Vaters wuchs noch kein graues Haar [. . .]. Er hatte Friedhöfe gemacht und machte der Frau schnell ein Kind. (*HT*, 20 f.)

That child, as is so often the case with the central figures of Müller's 'autofiktionale' writings, can be read as a surrogate version of the author herself; indeed, her whole aesthetic appears to be based on the assumption that readers will receive her works in this way.[5]

That both sections quoted here thematize forms of totalitarianism is clear from the outset, although in the first paragraph the narrator is unwilling to intrude to draw any explicit conclusions from what is being described. Nevertheless, the seemingly random details in the first passage still leave one with a sense of seediness and political apathy. The predictably mechanical routine with which Lola replaces the equally predictable speeches of the dictator, with the previous one being crumpled up and discarded as if as ephemeral as Lola's state stockings (the inferior 'Patentstrümpfe', notorious for their tendency to ladder at first wearing), may, in terms of body language, be comment enough on the fatuous promises of an improved standard of living offered in his speeches – especially since there appears to be no shortage of unwearable stockings with which to clean the glass panes. Tellingly, the reader has no evidence of interest on the part of Lola or the narrator in what the *Conducator* actually has to say in his public utterances. Instead attention rests on their having to be ritually displayed in the 'Studentenheim' and on what this implies about the totalitarian world the Ceauşescu-figure has created. Details, such as having to blow away the dead insects or the incident when Lola is spied on by a fellow student clearly eager to denounce her in the name of the collective, even the surreal image of Lola – soon to commit suicide – trapped, like the dead flies, in the hostel's propaganda display-case, all contribute to a bleak picture of senseless mundane activity and a world stifled by political rhetoric and empty promises. Even without the word 'Diktator', one would be left with a damning enough image of Lola's drab world, the very antithesis of the one the propaganda of the time was anxious to dangle in front of the Romanian people. The cleaning of the glass comes across as an institutional chore rather than as some token of political conviction or a gesture of social conscience; and in any case, the whole incident ends in bickering. As so often in *Herztier*, much remains 'zwischen den Sätzen': 'das Ausgelassene', in terms of the wider political context, is merely hinted at through such symptomatic details. However, what the narrator goes on to portray in the two paragraphs immediately following this early description of Lola no longer remains on the surface and without commentary. In fact, the second passage is politically far more controversial and prepares the ground for one of the most hard-hitting attacks on Romanian history as a vicious circle in the entire novel. The image of the Romanian-German father who was in the SS during the War and who, having returned home after what is here termed 'ein verlorener Krieg',[6] an ideological turncoat with a clean civilian shirt in the cupboard and not a single grey hair on his head, satirically sums up the typical attitude to the past of many in the older generation of Germans in the Banat and Transylvania. 'Er war singend in die Welt marschiert' (*HT*, 21), we are told. And he comes back unrepentant.

Müller's prose often presents the reader with images from the present day of ex-members of Romania's SS-units, largely drawn from the country's ethnic German communities, gathering to sing Nazi songs from their brief moment of glory: for instance, the 'Heimabende' recalled in *Der Teufel sitzt im Spiegel* and *In der Falle*. Usually nostalgia for the 'good old Nazi days' is coupled with reminders of the dark past that has been so conveniently glossed over: 'Er hatte in der Welt Friedhöfe gemacht und die Orte schnell verlassen' (*HT*, 21). The disturbing euphemism 'Friedhöfe machen' is repeated at a number of crucial points in *Herztier*; for example, we hear that Edgar's uncles 'hatten bei den Totenkopf-Verbänden Friedhöfe gemacht und trennten sich nach dem Krieg. Sie trugen im Schädel die gleiche Fracht' (*HT*, 65 f.). The general picture offered of the dwindling German minority is of a group of individuals still carrying around with them their burden of personal guilt for past crimes and yet continuing to display unreconstructed reactionary behaviour patterns. *Niederungen* had already evoked the stock figure of one of Hitler's willing executioners: 'Er war im Krieg. Für fünfundzwanzig Tote hat er eine Auszeichnung bekommen. Er hat mehrere Auszeichnungen mitgebracht' (*N*, 9), but it is only with *Herztier* that such references to people's pasts serve an essentially more critical purpose than merely reminding us of the fascist history of one of Romania's main ethnic minorities, important though that issue is in the work.[7] A passage concerned with the longing of the inhabitants of the area in general (not just the Germans) to escape from Ceaușescu's Romania – by swimming across the Danube 'bis das Wasser Ausland wird' or '[d]em Mais nachrennen, bis der Boden Ausland wird' (*HT*, 55 f.)

John J. White

– culminates in the observation that not all people share this urge
to risk their lives in a bid for freedom: 'Nur der Diktator und
seine Wächter wollten nicht fliehen [. . .]. Sie werden heute noch
und morgen wieder Friedhöfe machen mit Hunden und Kugeln'
(*HT*, 56). Again, restricting the phrase only to figures in
Ceauşescu's contemporary world and not to any crimes from the
Nazi past, the narrator goes on to declare: 'Und ich dachte mir,
daß alles etwas nützt, was denen schadet, die Friedhöfe machen'
(*HT*, 57 f.). In fact, the parallel between the present dictator's
henchmen 'die Friedhöfe machen' and those who did so with such
enthusiasm during the Second World War under Romania's pro-
German wartime dictatorship is a major feature of the novel's
narrative strategy, one intended to be particularly damaging to the
current regime.

There have been occasions when Müller's publicly expressed
views on political regimes of various hues and from different
periods of history have been vitiated by too totalizing an
approach, for instance when she declares: 'Nach allem, was ich
über den Nationalsozialismus, den Stalinismus, den post-
stalinistischen Sozialismus weiß, glaube ich, daß Menschen in allen
Diktaturen (so unterschiedlich sie auch sein mögen) vor ähnlichen
Grundsituationen stehen' (*FA*, 11). The failure of the all-purpose
term 'Diktatur' to differentiate between unlike forms of repressive
demagogic rule and various totalitarian forms of collective government from both the right and the left or between degrees of
coercion and conditioning under the various regimes she is com-
paring for critical purposes has on occasions undermined the
charges she was seeking to make. To claim of a heterogeneous
array of states that they are all equally characterized by a
'Todesangst, die ausgeht von politischer Macht, vom Staat und
seinen Apparaten. Verbrechen, institutionalisiert als Beruf, staatlich
gefördert, gedeckt und sogar belohnt' and that 'Solche Staaten
sind Diktaturen. Menschenleben werden offen unter die Erde
gebracht oder verstohlen, durch Zermürbung, nach innen gekippt'
(*FA*, 10) risks riding roughshod over crucial differences. On the
other hand, what is being presented by means of *Herztier*'s
'Friedhöfe machen' phrase is a much more controlled and hence
devastating juxtaposition than any such reductive analogy
between the regimes of Nicolae Ceauşescu and Ion Antonescu.
For it uses the suppressed history of the one regime as a stick
with which to beat the present of the other.

The underlying issues broached here were for many years taboo in post-war Romania, and for more reasons than the obvious danger that they risked reminding people of the extent to which history was repeating itself. Edgar's words in *Herztier* help set the repression under Ceauşescu in the historical context of the country's Second World War past during Antonescu's fascist military dictatorship and in doing so they relate the immediate predicament to a chapter of the nation's 'unbewältigte Vergangenheit'. Yet this is only part of the picture; the Ceauşescu–Antonescu parallel also touches on the thorny matter of the country's large ethnic minorities and the extent to which their very presence in Romania constituted an implied challenge to any cosmetic picture of national harmony and of a socialist state born out of the defeat of fascism by the forces of the left.

Although tensions caused by Romania's ethnic diversity were to remain a constant thorn in the side of Ceauşescu's regime, the minorities issue actually represented much older unfinished business left over, not just from the First World War, from the conditions imposed by the Versailles Treaty and disputes leading up to the Second World War and on to its aftermath, but from as far back as the Austro-Hungarian Empire of earlier centuries. So intractable was the whole question of the minority groups in the Romanian region that for many years after 1945 any talk of them as 'minorities' was prohibited. The whole vexed status of Romania's leading ethnic minorities, numbering from 200,000 Germans to as many as two million Magyars, their importance not just within internal Romanian politics, but also for the country's precarious relations with West Germany, Hungary and the USSR (from whom Ceauşescu wished to maintain his independence, with Western help), explains the caution with which the leadership had to treat the ethnicity issue. Officially, the land had to be presented as the epitome of harmony within diversity, with all ethnic minorities sharing some overriding 'Romanian' socialist identity.[8] However, for this to be possible, much of what had taken place in the not too distant past had to be either reinterpreted or conveniently forgotten: not just the behaviour of Codreanu's Iron Guards and of the German and Romanian fascists under Antonescu, but also the subsequent Stalinist measures (draconian agrarian collectivization, the enforced relocation of ethnic communities, slave-labour projects, as well as repeated flouting of the guarantees for minorities enshrined in the 1952 constitution),

all things that haunted the memories of the various ethnic communities in particular.[9] In the words of *Barfüßiger Februar*, a monumental 'Schweigen der rumänischen Geschichte' was the sole
foundation on which Ceauşescu's new society could be built (*BF*,
105). As is argued in *Hunger und Seide*, specifically with reference
to the hostilities in former Yugoslavia: 'Die Diktaturen haben,
solange sie funktionierten, die Minderheitenprobleme im Inneren
der Staaten durch den Würgegriff erstickt' (*HS*, 160).

What is being alluded to in such works as *Herztier*, then, is not
just individual amnesia about recent historical events (cf. *Herztier*'s
image 'der Vater steckt sein schlechtes Gewissen in die dümmsten
Pflanzen und hackt sie ab', *HT*, 21), but wholesale state manipulation of the past, as typified in the following official remarks from
the pen of Ceauşescu himself:

> Alongside the Romanian people have settled on large expanses in the
> course of centuries [. . .] Magyars, Germans and other nationalities;
> everything that has been build [sic] is the joint work of the Romanian,
> Magyar and German working people and of those of other national-
> ities who [. . .] benefit today from the results of the building of our
> new society.[10]

In *Herztier*, we hear a less anodyne account of one particular
German father's contribution to Romanian society: 'Auch mein
Vater war erwachsen [. . .], sonst wäre er nicht in der SS
gewesen. [. . .] Daß er nach dem Krieg politisch nicht mehr zu
gebrauchen war, das ist nicht seine Reue. Er war in die falsche
Richtung marschiert, das ist alles'. To which comes the reply: 'Als
Spitzel sind alle zu gebrauchen [. . .], ob sie bei Hitler oder
Antonescu waren [. . .]. Ein paar Jahre nach Hitler, weinten sie
alle um Stalin [. . .]. Seither helfen sie Ceauşescu Friedhöfe
machen' (*HT*, 183). While the names Hitler and Stalin here do little
more than align Ceauşescu with the standard archetypes of
despotic totalitarianism, the reference to Antonescu does particu-
larize a clichéd analogy by anchoring it within twentieth-century
Romanian history. That is to say, the fascist military dictatorship
of General (later Marshal) Ion Antonescu from 1940 to 1944, leading in 1941 to Romania's entering the war on the Axis side, was
an inglorious period in the history of the German ethnic minority,
with the German Romanians volunteering in droves for the SS and
the Swabian and Saxon communities of the Banat and

Transylvania largely in support, and seldom on the receiving end, of Antonescu's racist-nationalist policies. (*Eine warme Kartoffel ist ein warmes Bett* singles out one lone figure as 'einer der wenigen Rumäniendeutschen, die während des zweiten Weltkriegs nicht in der SS waren', and Richard Wagner, coming from the same background as Müller, has remarked: 'die Generation meines Vaters war zu 90% in der Waffen-SS'.)[11] While various unsuccessful campaigns were launched to rehabilitate Antonescu during the Ceauşescu regime, the fact remains that he was usually associated with the alliance with Nazi Germany rather than his later *volte-face*. Moreover, abortive attempts at a re-evaluation of his role in history were counterproductive, with the Romanian-Germans who had so enthusiastically supported the Axis alliance remaining suspect in the eyes of the socialist state as much for their contaminated past as for any present-day threat they represented.

By conjuring up various images of unregenerate ex-SS fathers, *Herztier* thus manages to transcend the immediate, essentially typological parallel between two totalitarian systems, one of the right, the other of the left, in order to show up the hypocrisy of the regime's propaganda image of multi-ethnic harmony in a country with such a divisive 'unbewältigte Vergangenheit'. The effect of such a pattern of analogies was also to place the novel within the wider context of contemporary West German 'Neue Subjektivität' by presenting the actions of *Herztier*'s equivalent of the *Aktionsgruppe Banat* within the framework of a by then familiar, historically motivated conflict between critical youth and reactionary parents.

Although the Antonescu–Ceauşescu regimes parallel is often introduced into Müller's works (usually not by actually naming Antonescu himself but simply by referring in generalized terms to the activities of his German henchmen), one would have to look long and hard for any mention of the ruthlessly Stalinist dictatorship of Gheorghe Gheorghiu-Dej which began in 1947 (with the declaration of a People's Republic) and lasted until 1965. Yet it must rate as the most repressively totalitarian episode in the country's entire history. This may partly be because Ceauşescu's victims, Müller's main focus, were hardly able to rise sufficiently above the considerable sufferings of the moment to be able to appreciate the finer differences between what one commentator has distinguished as the *terror* of the years under Dej and the widespread *fear*, but only that, characteristic of life under

Ceaușescu's *Securitate*.[12] However, the chief reason for Dej's absence, even as a folk memory, is probably the fact that his reign meant equal terror for all, Romanians and ethnic sub-groups alike. Under Ceaușescu, by contrast, ethnic minorities were specifically targeted as a divisive element in society and attacked as potential saboteurs or because of putative links with communities abroad (a key theme in *Heute wär ich mir lieber nicht begegnet*). Understandably, given that Müller grew up during a less terror-ridden period in Romania's history than had been experienced under Dej, she felt she had a right, in the context of the hopes for change aroused by *glasnost*, to view her own time with greater expectations than anyone could have dared entertain thirty years earlier. As Müller and Richard Wagner have emphasized, the *Aktionsgruppe Banat* viewed themselves as heirs to the legacy of 1968 and the Prague Spring.

A further hope-giving factor was the awareness that Ceaușescu's regime began with signs there would be a relaxation of the harshness experienced under Dej, not least because the country needed Western support to pursue its policy of relative independence from the Soviet Union and the other Warsaw Pact satellite states. Yet as far as the ethnic issue was concerned, the reality soon deteriorated. With a shared border with Hungary and mindful of a longstanding history of Magyar irredentism, the regime showed insensitivity in its treatment of its large Hungarian minority, mainly settled in Transylvania, with any vestige of a minorities policy lurching from crisis to crisis until the attempted arrest of the Magyars' spiritual leader, Pastor Tokes, sparked off the events of 1989.[13] Cognate problems of a lesser magnitude were caused by a substantial Russian minority in Moldova (Bessarabia) and the Ruthenians of the Bukovina. However, the situation of the ethnic Germans differed substantially in many respects from that of any other ethnic minority groups in Romania, not only because of the past, but in respect of the economic influence and moral pressure a country as powerful as West Germany could exert over the Ceaușescu regime.

The minorities problem and its political ramifications were bound to play a major role as background to the work of a critically minded German-Romanian writer; and when treated as the source of tension that it in reality was, rather than as an excuse for indulging in some kind of·cloying *Heimatliteratur*, it could become an effective source of attack on the regime. So too could another phenomenon: its policy of releasing members of the German minority to the Federal Republic for hard currency (the infamous 'Kopfgeld'). After the clandestine agreement between Bonn and Bucharest of 1967, some 200,000 ethnic German 'Aussiedler' left Romania over the next two decades. The very existence of this undignified barter in human lives put a large question mark against the regime's own self-presentation, as well as creating further friction between the various ethnic groups. The way in which it was administered, in both Romania and the receiving countries, could not fail to arouse memories of other transactions during the Third Reich. Richard Wagner's *Begrüßungsgeld* and Müller's *Reisende auf einem Bein* register the complex feelings and experiences of those arriving in the West as a result of such an opportunistic policy, while their *Ausreiseantrag* and *Der Mensch ist ein großer Fasan auf der Welt*, respectively, give some sense of the corruption and chicanery that the process of obtaining the right documents and making the travel arrangements involved. In fact, totalitarianism as bureaucracy is as much a part of Müller's picture of the Ceaușescu regime as it is of Hitler's Germany, even if *Herztier* does give the impression of there being a substantial difference between the Third Reich's relatively efficient machine and the dilapidated Gogolian bureaucracies of contemporary Eastern Europe, where a combination of corruption and crass incompetence adds to the would-be emigrants' sufferings. Not surprisingly, these features of what H. G. Adler has referred to as the administration ('Verwaltung') of human beings under totalitarianism[14] is also a major theme in Müller's fiction.

'Wie beschreibt man eine Diktatur?' was one of the questions Müller posed in the discussion following a reading from *Reisende auf einem Bein* at Swansea in the autumn of 1996. One solution, according to her, could be to focus on 'Männer und Frauen im Alltag', the 'Alltag' of totalitarianism. In doing so, she has frequently sought to refrain from too much specificity. As she once said in another interview about the central figure of *Reisende auf einem Bein*:

Ich wollte mit der Person von Irene von mir selber weggehen und verallgemeinern. Aus diesem Grund habe ich beispielsweise vermieden, Rumänien im Buch zu nennen. Ihre Situation trifft auf viele zu, die etwa aus Ländern aus dem Osten hierherkommen. Ich hätte am liebsten auch die politischen Gründe des Weggehens von Irene ausgespart, aber das konnte ich nicht, ich habe gesehen, daß ich ohne diese politische Dimension nicht auskomme.[15]

Nevertheless, here as elsewhere, Müller has seldom been able to avoid the specifically Romanian 'political dimension' completely. Indeed, it is not difficult to abstract from her fiction and essays a whole range of examples of the abuse of human rights under the Ceauşescus and of the extent to which political control permeated daily life. I am thinking of such things as the destruction of privacy in the interests of political surveillance: the intrusive presence of the Party's loudspeakers in public places (*HT*, 26), and the ubiquitous propaganda slogans and pictures of the leader (*FJ*, 84, 103). We hear much of the role of the state's strenuous anti-abortion campaign (*HS*, 78 ff.) where, with an illegally terminated pregnancy equatable with treason, gynaecologists would, under the pretext of health check-ups, be in a position to monitor patients for symptoms of pregnancy and denounce them if any irregularities appeared. This is one of those calculatedly demeaning forms of 'Alltagsfaschismus' where a massive intrusion into people's private lives may be as important as a symbolic demonstration of totalitarian power as an end in itself. Clearly, a large proportion of Romania's population was in some respect implicated in such a pervasive state system of 'Verwaltung'. Victims are difficult to keep separate from perpetrators: 'Der Fuchs war damals schon der Jäger'.

In both the fiction and essayistic writings, we repeatedly encounter evidence of a world in which any 'Suche nach Menschenwürde [. . .] zur Straftat erklärt [wird]' (*FA*, 11) and the *Securitate*'s opening of private correspondence is accepted by the state as a matter of course (*HT*, 90). We hear of prohibitions on allegedly seditious gatherings, including even weddings in the case of suspected dissidents (*FJ*, 230), of a climate of suspicion in which contact with the West can be seen as a form of 'Prostitution' or even 'Landesverrat' (*HB*, 57), and the accused letter-writer can be dismissed from work on trumped-up charges. (The exaggerated role played by success in sport within the official media, *HS*, 20 f., is obviously meant to divert public awareness from the country's isolationist policies, as is the misappropriation of 'Internationaler Frauentag' for agitational purposes, *KB*, 76, and *HS*, 102 ff.) The regular use, or threat, of interrogation combined with violence is seen to rule many people's lives. This is particularly true of *Heute wär ich mir lieber nicht begegnet*, where we receive the most detailed psychological picture of just what 'Demütigung' does to the victim: 'Wenn ich zum Verhör gehe, muß ich das Glück von vornherein zu Hause lassen' (*HB*, 22); it is as if 'man sich am ganzen Körper barfuß fühlt' (*HB*, 10). The arranged 'Verkehrsunfälle' used by the *Securitate* as a cover for the elimination of those who had become inconvenient are recalled in *Hunger und Seide*: 'Und es gab sie im Land, diese Toten: Streikanführer aus dem Schiltal, denen Ceauşescu persönlich Straffreiheit versprochen hatte, starben bei Verkehrsunfällen. Und es gab Fensterstürze, Erhängte und Ertrunkene und Vergiftete gab es. Angeblich Suizide. Immer ohne Obduktion schnell ins Grab gelegt' (*HS*, 98); and they also figure among Major Alba's threats to the central figure in *Heute wär ich mir lieber nicht begegnet* (e.g. *HB*, 141). Yet it is not only individual safety which is threatened: we hear of 'ethnic cleansing' by means of the moving of minorities to predominantly Romanian areas (for example the soldiers and those engaged in state construction projects in *Herztier*). The curtailment of an entire nation's freedom of movement, with the bodies of those who unsuccessfully attempt to escape being brought back in secret each night (*FJ*, 245) or being washed downriver the next morning, becomes a recurrent motif in Müller's works. Lilli's abortive attempt to escape to Hungary plays an important role in the interrogations in *Heute wär ich mir lieber nicht begegnet*, and even those who reach the West by other less dangerous means have many hazards to overcome, hence the residual fear of all people in uniforms, even the local postman (*FJ*, 256 f.). In the context of such a widespread 'Überwachungssystem', the fact that large portions of the population can be assumed to be informants inevitably plays on the individual's sense of integrity and progressively corrodes personal relationships (*In der Falle* even refers to 'die persönliche Paranoia als Schutz in der Totalität einer paranoiden Umgebung', *FA*, 35). Legalized abuse of power at a national level is shown to assume a variety of bizarre forms, from the arbitrary imposition of a 'Schornsteinsteuer' (*N*, 82) to the unrealistic pressures on collective farms to maximize production beyond the feasible, despite being established on poor soil (*N*, 125). The hypocrisy, for a self-proclaimed socialist society, of the good life and privileges of the *nomenklatura* (cf. 'Die stillen Straßen der Macht', *FJ*, 31 ff.) is probably less important in itself than because of the effect it has on those who have continually to live in poverty or work at a Stakhanovite pace to bolster up an inefficient economy.

As a writer, Müller has always remained particularly sensitive to the intrusive forms of 'Sprachregelung' practised in totalitarian states (cf. *KB*, 14, and *HS, passim*). Thus, in *Heute wär ich mir lieber nicht begegnet* the state's stultifyingly jargon-ridden language is attacked as 'eine Sprache, in der es nie ums Riechen und Schmecken ging, nie ums Hören und Sehen' (*HB*, 100), an observation which clearly has implications for the sensual quality of her own writing.

Above all in her essayistic recollections, Müller pays particular attention to the importance of the whims and eccentricities of the dictator-figure himself and the ludicrous forms which these take: an example is the removal of all poultry and dogs from any town where Ceauşescu was scheduled to spend the night ('Nur das Licht darf den Diktator wecken [. . .], das Krähen und Bellen macht ihn unberechenbar', *FJ*, 238 f.). Or the strategic positioning of selected high quality dairy cattle, so-called 'Präsidentenkühe', to be seen on his official visits to agricultural communities to give 'der geliebteste Sohn des Volkes' the impression of a blooming farming economy (*HS*, 11). At one point in 'Hunger und Seide. Männer und Frauen im Alltag', Müller talks about the personality cult in Ceauşescu's Romania:

> Durch den Personenkult waren Ceauşescu und seine Ehefrau die einzigen Herrschenden im Land. Alle anderen Mächtigen waren auch Untertanen. Sie mußten die Macht des Herrscherpaares vertreten. Sie mußten sich, in allem, was sie sagten, auf das Herrscherpaar beziehen. Sie mußten die Sprache des Herrscherpaares wiederkäuen. Deshalb war ihre Sprache die deutlichste Untertanensprache in diesem Land. So wie die Menschen, die die leeren Gänge in den Blicken und auf der Haut Kolonnenkleider trugen, durch ausländische Zigarettenpäckchen und Feuerzeuge und Kugelschreiber die Selbstverständlichkeiten der Mächtigen berühren wollten, so eigneten sie sich auch, oft unbewußt, deren Sprache an. (*HS*, 76 f.)

This symbiotic relationship between dictator and subject – mirrored in that between interrogator and person interrogated – is central to Müller's presentation of the *Conducator*'s place and function within one particular totalitarian system. The national dictator (or 'Herrscherpaar', in this case, although little attention is paid to the specific repercussions of such a unique duumvirate) breeds

mini-dictators, who seek their legitimacy in mimicking the des-
pot's behaviour. That such a well-orchestrated and pervasive
'Personenkult' is not to be confused with a situation where, to use
Tom Gallagher's words, the leader can in retrospect be 'blamed
for the faults of an entire system',[16] is made clear even in the
above passage. But as the 'Als Spitzel sind alle zu gebrauchen'
remark implies, regimes depend on acts of complicity and on
people's willingness to compromise, not just on coercive brutality
or the chameleon principle of power.

On the whole, the fiction's picture of totalitarianism as experienced by individual fictive characters might be thought of as dis-
playing a penchant for the anecdotal. It could even be argued that
such a tendency reflects the experiences of people actually living
under such a system. But there are on occasions more specific
theoretical reasons for Müller's approach, and they relate to the
perceived need to counter ideological systematization with the
randomness of untheorized experience and to stress the incidental
rather than the ideologically structured. In this connection, one of
Herta Müller's most important theoretical statements about her
conception of totalitarianism and of the subject's importance for
her literary and other writings is to be found in her 1994 paper
'Zehn Finger sind keine Utopie', published the following year in
Hunger und Seide. Here, she sets out a critique of virtually all
forms of totalitarianism as in essence 'angewandte Utopien': mis-
guided attempts at regimenting society in the name of an abstract
utopian goal with (in her eyes) inevitably disastrous consequences.
The state's imposition of a systematic ideology on people in the
name of such ideals is presented as a procrustean programme that
inevitably ends up allowing system to prevail over detail and the
ends to justify the means:

> Die Ideologie des Sozialismus war eine angewandte Utopie. Die
> angewandte Utopie ergab eine Diktatur. Jede Utopie, die das Papier
> verläßt und sich zwischen Menschen stellt, uniformiert die nackte
> Unzähligkeit der Versuche, ein Leben zu finden, das man aushält,
> [. . .] der Sozialismus war nicht der Sozialismus gewesen. Es war
> angeblich etwas ganz anderes, was so viele Menschen im Namen einer
> Idee gedemütigt, beschädigt, zerbrochen oder getötet hat. Es war dies
> eine Namensfälschung. (*HS*, 50 f.)

For that 'something else', Müller uses a variety of names: 'System',
'das Ganze', 'Kontrolle des Bewußtseins', or most frequently

'Diktatur', as well as occasionally 'der totalitäre Staat' (e.g. *TS*, 21). However, what is of overriding importance here is less her bleak equation of *all* attempts to achieve some form of more egalitarian society with dictatorship than the premisses upon which her argument is based and the consequences she draws from such a position. These include the following: (i) that it is not just the methods of socialism's attempt at achieving communism that are wrong, but the underlying assumption that everyone should be striving after the same goal: 'Es gibt keinen Zustand, in dem das Wort Glück für viele Menschen das gleiche bedeutet. Es sollte diesen Zustand nicht geben' (*HS*, 53). In elaborating on this point, the various essays in *Hunger und Seide* posit parallels between the overt brutality of Ceauşescu's Romania and various other socialist regimes, and even between the methods of 'Bewußtseinskontrolle' practised by the Church and those of state totalitarianism. ('Der Glaube an Gott ist die erste Utopie, vor der ich versagt habe. Und die zweite ist die Utopie vom Glück des Volkes in einer hellen Zukunft', *HS*, 54.) (ii) that the main stumbling block is not the disparity between ends and means, but between procrustean theory and the intractable nature of the world we live in: 'Wenn alle Dinge, zwischen denen man steht, so viele Böden haben, dann fehlt einem nicht auch noch der sekundäre Guß darüber, die Theorie' (*HS*, 54). Theory is axiomatically rejected as a misconstrued attempt at systematizing reality at the cognitive level, that is, even before it is applied by dictators to the reality which they wish to control in the name of any unattainable reality they wish to construct. (iii) that the answer to totalitarianism *qua* ideology is not a counter-ideology, but *no* ideology: 'Um gegen eine Diktatur zu sein, um sich in Distanz zu ihr zu begeben [and this idea applies to her writing in Romania before 1987 as much as to the later works], brauchte ich keinen Glauben an die ideale andere Gesellschaft' (*HS*, 53). (iv) that there is a symmetry between totalitarianism's disdain for the individual and any system's treatment of recalcitrant details: 'Meine Einzelheiten hatten keine Gültigkeit, sie waren nicht ein Teil, sondern ein Feind des Ganzen. Wer wie ich damit anfing, in Einzelheiten zu leben, brachte das Ganze nie zusammen. Wer im Detail leben mußte, stellte nur Hürden auf für das Ganze' (*HS*, 59). This in due course leads to the emphatic resolution: 'Leben wir also im Detail' (*HS*, 61). Totalitarianism is consequently to be presented in Müller's fiction and essays, if it is to be countered, via its 'Einzelheiten', organized in superimposed aesthetic patterns rather than ideological interpretive and manipulative systems. When Major Alba says to the protagonist of *Heute wär ich mir lieber nicht begegnet*, 'Siehst du, die Dinge verbinden sich', her revealing reply is: 'Bei Ihnen, bei mir nicht' (*HB*, 28, cf. also 35).

The opposite of political systematizing is the subject and his or her respect for 'die Einzelheiten'. In the words of *In der Falle*: 'Der literarische Text [. . .] allein schafft es, durch das Detail der Sinne, die Vorstellbarkeit des Ganzen zu erzwingen. Er stellt den persönlichen Blickfang, das einzelne Befinden über die Geschichtsschreibung, die sich dem Nachempfinden des einzelnen Unglücks verschließt' (*FA*, 5). Or to look at it another way, in such a scheme, the opposite of totalitarianism is taken to be individualism.

The contributions by Margaret Littler and Brigid Haines to the present volume and Brigid Haines's article 'Subjectivity (un)-bound' raise the central question of the relationship of Herta Müller's conception of the subject to the anti-totalitarian strategy advocated in 'Zehn Finger sind keine Utopie'. In 'Beyond Alienation', Littler writes of the present as a 'time when the beleaguered subject of modernity has been displaced by a fragmented, discursively contested and sexually differentiated subject'.[17] Her exploration of the 'postmodern subjects' of Müller's fiction, in particular *Reisende auf einem Bein*, explores the extent to which 'chaotic urban diversity' might be regarded as 'intrinsic' to such a fragmented subjectivity.[18] When set alongside Moníková, Müller is judged to be 'the writer who departs more radically from notions of rational subjectivity'.[19] Littler's contention – that it is above all the city that 'poses a challenge to the conscious subject's integrity'[20] – nevertheless still holds available the implication that it is specifically the *Western* city, indeed the 'pluralist' West in general, that functions as the ultimate 'prerequisite for the postmodern experience of city life'.[21] However, the notion of the subject's 'integrity' which becomes increasingly important in the concluding section of Littler's argument possesses a dual connotation. First, it means wholeness (the opposite, in other words, of postmodern fragmentation); second, it in many contexts also refers to a specifically *ethical* form of integrity (without compromise, with a clear agenda and an underlying value-centre). Littler's concluding reference to the problem of 'constant negotiation between the *theoretical* affirmation of fragmentation [. . .] and the *political* need to occupy positions of real subjective agency'[22] does, although expressed in largely feminist terms, put its finger on a wider issue of vital importance to any assessment of what Brigid Haines refers to as Müller's 'micro-politics of resistance':[23] that is, the question of the kind of subject that is the prerequisite for effective resistance and as a value-centre for dissident literature.

What Littler, from the perspective of *Reisende auf einem Bein*, sees as a 'constant negotiation' between two conceptions of the subject gains from being treated phaseologically in Haines's 'Subjectivity (un)bound'. Positing a 'return to centredness' in Müller's prose of the 1990s, in particular in the last three novels (*Der Fuchs war damals schon der Jäger*, *Herztier* and *Heute wär ich mir lieber nicht begegnet*), Haines restores a political meaning to the notion of the subject's integrity and to 'im Detail leben' as a response to totalitarianism.[24] Hence, despite numerous aesthetic gestures on Müller's part towards the earlier premiss of a deconstructed subject, a more essentialist view of the subject – theorized more unequivocally in *In der Falle* than anywhere in *Hunger und Seide* – comes to the fore. On such a reading of Müller's development, there is not only a certain coherence between the recent fiction and her essayistic publications, the very presence of such a body of for the large part political essayism becomes more understandable.

Even to periodize Müller's treatment of the decentred and recentred self, in the way that 'Subjectivity (un)bound' does, still leaves various issues related to her response to totalitarianism unresolved, not least the actual relationship of 'Zehn Finger sind keine Utopie' to the two phases. The anti-system thrust to *Hunger und Seide*'s 'Ideologieverdacht' and its espousal of 'im Detail Leben' as a narrative strategy might in some respects seem more in keeping with Müller's aesthetic up to *Reisende auf einem Bein*; on the other hand, the 'micro-politics of resistance' promulgated in *Hunger und Seide* and *In der Falle* and the return to a different conception of the self that Haines has detected in recent years still remains less consistently in evidence in the fiction of the period than the theory might have led one to expect. It is as if the dominant pattern of interplay between the private and the political in *Heute wär ich mir lieber nicht begegnet* were paradigmatic of Müller's current predicament: for just as in that novel the personal sphere never proves to be capable of insulation from the domain of Major Alba and narrative recollections of seemingly innocent events are suddenly invaded by thoughts about the next interrogation or memories of past ones, so virtually all of Müller's strategies of literary resistance end up demonstrating her inability 'ohne die [. . .] politische Dimension [auszukommen]'. Not just because her literary works have shown that resistance to totalitarianism axiomatically has to be a political, if not an ideological, activity, but also because, as her recently formulated conception of the writer's integrity makes clear, the kind of subject needed as a counter to totalitarianism is something remote from postmodernism by virtue of its concern with 'persönliche Integrität', 'moralische Maßstäbe' and an exemplary 'Menschenbild' (*FA*, 6). Whether this is merely a necessary rhetorical construct[25] to set against totalitarianism (something akin to the strategic essentialism that Gayatri Chakravorty Spivak has advocated in *In Other Worlds*[26] and elsewhere) or whether the exile writer has radically shifted her position is not easy to determine. And in any case, thematic pressures differentiating works set in Ceaușescu's Romania from those (few) dealing primarily with the experience of the West would also have to be taken into account when trying to establish whether there is a consistent paradigm-change in Müller's recent writings. A more detailed comparison of the thematized subject in *Heute wär ich mir lieber nicht begegnet* and that of *Reisende auf einem Bein* would be required to gauge the true extent to which the fiction is lagging behind the goal set out in *In der Falle*. What is beyond dispute, however, is the fact that, despite repeated attempts to emancipate herself from the hold totalitarianism continues to have on the writings she has produced since her move to the West in 1987, Herta Müller has as a writer been unable to break free from her past in the way that Richard Wagner, for example, has. She has remained 'in der Falle' – totalitarianism's trap.

Notes

[1] '"Und ist der Ort, wo wir leben"'. Schreiben aus Unzufriedenheit. Gespräch mit der Schriftstellerin Herta Müller', *Die Woche*, 2 April 1982.
[2] Norbert Otto Eke, '"Überall, wo man den Tod gesehen hat"'. Zeitlichkeit und Tod in der Prosa Herta Müllers. Anmerkungen zu einem Motivzusammenhang', in Norbert Otto Eke (ed.), *Die erfundene Wahrnehmung. Annäherung an Herta Müller* (Paderborn, Igel Verlag, 1991), 74–94, here 90.

³ 'Kultur: Briefe. Richard Wagner, Berlin', *Literatur und Kritik*, 283–84 (April, 1994), 11 f., 11.
⁴ 'Bewohner mit Handgepäck. Aus dem Banat nach Berlin ausgewandert. Die Schriftstellerin Herta Müller im Gespräch [mit Walter Vogl]', *Die Presse*, 7 January 1989.
⁵ See her introductory remarks concerning the authors discussed in *In der Falle*: 'Die Bücher, von denen ich reden will, sind mit einem sehr hohen Preis (meist mit einem zu hohen) von ihren Autoren bezahlt worden. Daher sind sie nicht bloß *Literatur* [. . .]. Sie sind mehr als das, weil gleichzeitig Beweis für die persönliche Integrität schreibender Personen. Sie stellen ohne Fingerzeig moralische Maßstäbe vor Augen, die unter drastischem, politischem Druck, in Situationen der Lebensbedrohung, nicht aufgegeben worden sind' (*FA*, 6).
⁶ In actual fact, Antonescu's hitherto fascist Romania found it politic suddenly to change sides and participate in its own 'liberation' by the Red Army at a certain stage of the Soviet advance westwards. Hence, in *Heute wär ich mir lieber nicht begegnet*, the narrator's objection to the implications of the state's annual August celebration of a so-called 'Tag der Befreiung' (*HB*, 49). See also Müller's bitter confession in *In der Falle*: 'Mir stand auch mein SS-Vater im Schädel. Und die vielen Deutschen, die fünfzig Jahre nach Kriegsende immer noch von ihrer Niederlage redeten' (*FA*, 40). For further details on this subject, see Antje Harnisch's highly informative '"Ausländerin im Ausland". Herta Müllers *Reisende auf einem Bein*', *Monatshefte*, 89 (1997), 507–20.
⁷ Having at one stage evoked a detailed picture of her ex-SS father as 'für mich das erste Beispiel von einem zuerst ahnungslos und später dumpf und gleichgültig [. . .] mitschuldig gewordenen Menschen', Müller goes on to remark: 'Mein Vater hatte im Krieg soviel gesungen, wie er geschossen hatte. Wenn die heimgekehrten SS-Soldaten, wie er, betrunken waren, sangen sie ihre stampfenden, draufgängerischen Lieder, die sie damals um ihr Leben gesungen hatten. Die zerfallene "Kameradschaft" war wieder da. Sie warfen sich in den Rausch einer derben Gemeinsamkeit. Die damit verbundenen Verbrechen blendeten sie aus' (*FA*, 8, 21).
⁸ This whole issue is treated in detail, with particular emphasis on Romania's cultural policy towards its ethnic minorities, in Katherine Verdery, *National Ideology under Socialism: Identity and Cultural Politics in Ceauşescu's Romania* (Berkeley; Los Angeles; London, University of California Press, 1991).
⁹ Although not extending to the period depicted in Müller's fiction, Robert R. King's *Minorities under Communism: Nationalities as a Source of Tension among the Balkan Communist States* (Cambridge/Mass., Harvard University Press, 1973) remains the classic treatment of this topic.
¹⁰ *Romania on the Way of* [sic] *Building up the Multilaterally Developed Socialist Society*, vol. 6 (Bucharest, Meridiane, 1972), 190.
¹¹ *KB*, 65 f.; Wagner, quoted from Susanne Broos, 'Richard Wagner: Politik ist immer eine Dimension in meinem Schreiben', *Börsenblatt für den deutschen Buchhandel*, 87 No. 2 (2 November 1993), 20.

[12] Dennis Deletant, *Ceauşescu and the 'Securitate': Coercion and Dissent in Romania, 1965–1989* (London, Hurst, 1995), 1 f.

[13] For details, in particular the role of a shared border with Hungary as a key factor, see Tom Gallagher, 'Communism and co-inhabiting nationalities', in Tom Gallagher, *Romania after Ceauşescu* (Edinburgh, Edinburgh University Press, 1995), 48–54.

[14] Section Six ('Der verwaltete Mensch') of Adler's *Der verwaltete Mensch. Studien zur Deportation der Juden aus Deutschland* (Tübingen, J. C. B. Mohr, 1974), a study which is generally far wider in scope than its title suggests, could with profit be applied to many regulatory features of the Ceauşescu regime.

[15] 'Die Verweigerung, sich verfügbar zu machen. Herta Müller und Richard Wagner im Gespräch [mit Bruno Preisendörfer]', *Zitty*, 26 (1989), 69.

[16] Gallagher, *Romania after Ceauşescu*, 67.

[17] See this volume, 36.

[18] Ibid., 40.

[19] Ibid.

[20] Ibid., 49.

[21] Ibid., 52.

[22] Ibid., 53.

[23] See Brigid Haines's contribution to this volume.

[24] Brigid Haines, 'Subjectivity (un)bound: Libuşe Moníková and Herta Müller', in Keith Bullivant, Geoffrey Giles and Walter Pape (eds.), *Germany and Eastern Europe 1870–1996* (Berlin, de Gruyter, 1998) (forthcoming).

[25] 'Zehn Finger sind keine Utopie' was originally delivered at the 'Glanz und Elend der Utopie' symposium (Glauchau, 1994). All quotations from this essay are taken from the version printed in *Hunger und Seide*, 50–61.

[26] Gayatri Chakravorty Spivak, *In Other Worlds: Essays in Cultural Politics* (New York; London, Routledge, 1988).

8

»Ein Platz für die Moral?« Herta Müller, ihre Texte und das poetische Moment

DAGMAR VON HOFF

Bevor ich auf Herta Müller und ihre Texte eingehen werde, möchte ich etwas Allgemeines zum Moralbegriff sagen. Dies deshalb, weil ich meine, daß diese Autorin, wie kaum eine andere in der deutschsprachigen Gegenwartsliteratur, einen moralischen Standpunkt behauptet, der für uns, die sich für frei halten, von großem Interesse sein sollte. Denn Freiheit muß vorausgesetzt werden, wenn Moralität möglich sein soll, denn diese meint Selbstgesetzgebung und Selbstausführung des Selbstgesetzten. Herta Müller produziert ihre Texte nicht im Elfenbeinturm, sondern entwickelt ihre literarischen Texte und ihre Essays aus einer engagierten Zeitzeugenschaft heraus. Und sie entwirft in diesen Texten einen Moment des Widerstands, nämlich vorzugehen gegen Situationen, die so unerträglich sind, daß man versuchen muß, sie zu ändern, ganz gleich, was aus einem selbst wird – so hat es einmal Theodor W. Adorno für die Aktion des 20. Juli definiert.[1] Ich möchte im folgenden – um dieses geradezu irrationale Element im moralischen Handeln zu erläutern – von einem normativen Moralbegriff, wie ihn Tzvetan Todorov verwendet, ausgehen, um dann in einem nächsten Schritt die moralische Kategorie um das Moment der Selbstreflexion zu erweitern, wie es Adorno vorschlägt. Danach sollen literarische Texte, aber auch Zeitungsartikel und Essays der Autorin Herta Müller herangezogen werden, um die Vielfalt ihrer poetischen Bezüge zur Moral vorzustellen.

Ein Platz für die Moral?

Die Frage: »Ein Platz für die Moral?« ist Todorovs Buch *Angesichts des Äußersten* entnommen, in dem er sich u.a. mit zwei Fragen auseinandersetzt: zum einen, ob Moral sich unter extremen und traumatisierenden Bedingungen auflöst, zum anderen, ob die Menschen – in den nationalsozialistischen Konzentrationslagern und den Lagern des Gulag – einen gnadenlosen Überlebenskrieg führen, einen Krieg aller gegen alle.[2] An diesem so oft und sehr schnell zitierten Gesetz des Dschungels – wie es auch in Berichten von Überlebenden der nationalsozialistischen und kommunistischen Lager formuliert wurde, z.B. Primo Levi, Überlebender von Auschwitz, in *Ist das ein Mensch?* (1961) – meldet Todorov aber schon sehr schnell Zweifel an. Denn derselbe Levi, der im Lager nur den erschöpfenden Kampf aller gegen alle sah, hatte geschrieben: »Alle sind sie Feinde oder Rivalen«, als er innehielt und sagte: »Aber nein«,[3] und er bemerkte, daß sie weder das eine noch das andere sind. Und Levi gibt dann eine Reihe von Beispielen, die dem Hobbes'schen Gesetz, bei dem der Mensch zum Wolf wird, widersprechen. Todorov verweist darauf, daß die Berichte der Überlebenden Auskunft darüber geben, daß Extremsituationen und Gewissen zusammenzudenken sind, daß selbst unter den unmenschlichsten Bedingungen noch ein moralisches Leben aufrechterhalten wurde, daß es eine Möglichkeit zu wählen gab.[4] Zu dieser Möglichkeit der Entscheidung schreibt Jorge Semprun, der Buchenwald überlebte:

> Im Lager wird der Mensch zu einem Tier, das fähig ist, einem Kameraden das letzte Brot wegzustehlen, das fähig ist, ihn in den Tod zu treiben. Im Lager wird der Mensch andererseits auch zu jenem unbesiegbaren Wesen, das fähig ist, den letzten Zigarettenstummel, das letzte Stück Brot, den letzten Atemzug zu teilen, um seinem Kameraden zu helfen.[5]

Die Entscheidung zugunsten der moralischen Qualitäten wird bei Semprun und bei Todorov aber nicht etwa idealisiert oder als Loblied des Leidens interpretiert, das Tugenden hervorbringt. Sondern es wird versucht, an kleinen menschlichen Gesten und Entscheidungen zu zeigen, inwieweit menschliche Würde selbst unter extremen gesellschaftlichen Bedingungen Wirkungen entfalten kann. Es ist also nicht die eindimensionale Welt der heroischen oder heiligen Haltung – die in Mut und Feigheit, Held und Verräter, Schwarz und Weiß unterscheidet[6] – die Todorov interessiert, sondern es ist vielmehr die Kraft eines Individuums, das entgegen aller Widerstände eine persönliche Entscheidung für das moralische Moment treffen will, ohne sie ideologisch zu legitimieren und/oder phantasmatisch abzusichern.

Der Begriff des Moralischen – den Todorov uneingeschränkt positiv benutzt – hat für uns häufig einen negativen Beiklang, verbindet er sich doch häufig mit der Vorstellung des Rigorismus, der konventionellen Enge und der Anpassung. Dennoch macht es Sinn, über die praktische und theoretische Dimension der Moral nachzudenken – denn sie versteht sich nicht von selbst. Theodor W. Adorno hat in seinen moralphilosophischen Vorlesungen, die er 1963 gehalten hat, und die 1996 erschienen sind, auf das Problem verwiesen, daß die Abwertung des Moralbegriffs als moralistisch und anachronistisch etwas unterschlägt, nämlich die Nivellierung der Problematik von Moral auf Ethik. Das entscheidende Moment der Moral, nämlich das Verhältnis des einzelnen Individuums zu dem Allgemeinen, werde dann nicht mehr erörtert. Während Moral vom lateinischen Wort mores – also von Sitte – abhängt, verweist Ethos auf die Vorstellung von Wesensart und damit auf einen weiten Begriff.[7] Geht es in der Ethik um die Vorstellung von Selbstverwirklichung *im allgemeinen Sinn*, so verlangt die Frage nach der Moral einen selbstkritischen und verantwortlichen Gestus beim *Individuum*, nämlich die Antwort auf die Frage Immanuel Kants: »Was soll ich tun?«[8]

Klima der Angst und moralische Dilemmata

Und an diesem Punkt setzen Herta Müllers Essays und literarische Texte ein. Nicht das unmittelbare So-Sein, sondern die Frage des richtigen Tuns wird als menschliche Konstellation diskutiert. Dies wird bei Herta Müller nicht in der Weise ausgedrückt, daß sie uns den Typus eines modernen Helden vor Augen führt, der sich politisch und moralisch korrekt verhält. Aber auch nicht in der Form, daß sie uns – wie Antonio Tabucchi in *Erklärt Pereira* (1994) – eine Hauptfigur entwirft, die in Zeiten der Diktatur (bei Tabucchi das Portugal Salazars in den 30er Jahren) sich von einer indolenten Natur zu einem engagierten Menschen entwickelt. Für Herta Müllers literarische Texte könnte man mit Adorno formulieren, daß sie einen »Widerhall des Grauens« erzeugen. Sie zeigt die Erfahrungen des Leids, die Beschädigungen, die ein totalitäres Regime beim Einzelnen physisch und psychisch hervorruft. Ihre Helden existieren im Klima der Angst. Dabei löst ihre Literatur eine realistische Schreibweise durch assoziierte Montage auf, in der Wirklichkeitspartikel neben Erinnerungen, Gedanken, Bildern und Träumen stehen. Das Verhältnis des einzelnen Individuums zum Allgemeinen entwerfen Müllers Texte in einer anderen Weise, als wir es von vielen Verarbeitungsstrategien und erprobten Schreibweisen her kennen, die den Faschismus behandeln. Sie knüpft weniger an exemplarische Texte, wie Anna Seghers' *Siebtes Kreuz*, Günter Grass' *Blechtrommel* oder Peter Weiss' *Ermittlung* an – sondern stellt für ihr Schreiben eine differente Traditionslinie her, indem sie sich in ihren Essays und Rezensionen auf Ruth Klüger, Georges-Arthur Goldschmidt, Inge Müller, Rolf Bossert, Jorge Semprun, Paul Celan bezieht – um nur einige zu nennen.[9]

Festzuhalten ist aber, daß Herta Müllers fiktionale Texte different zu ihren Essays sind (vgl. ihre beiden Essaybände *Hunger und Seide* (1995) und *Der Teufel sitzt im Spiegel* (1991) sowie ihre Beiträge in Zeitungen). In ihren Artikeln und essayistischen Werken äußert sie sich sehr viel deutlicher zu politischen Fragen und zum Tagesgeschehen und weist auf die Gleichgültigkeit und Gedankenlosigkeit unserer westlichen Gesellschaft hin. So sind es gerade auch moralische Dilemmata, die sie in ihren Essays scharf und deutlich formuliert. In einem Artikel in der *Frankfurter Allgemeinen Zeitung* hat sie sich u.a. mit einem bundesrepublikanischen Phänomen auseinandergesetzt, nämlich dem, allzuschnell Verständnis für opportunistische Haltungen, für den typischen Mitläufer im totalitären System aufzubringen. »Ich weiß nicht, wie ich mich in der Diktatur (und hier könnte man den Nationalsozialismus, aber auch die DDR einsetzen) verhalten hätte?«[10] läßt sie eine Freundin sagen. Doch was wird da eigentlich gesagt? Daß man nicht so sicher ist, demokratische Maßstäbe über Bord zu werfen, wenn diktatorische Spielregeln herrschen? Und das Besondere von Herta Müllers kurzer Intervention für das Demokratieverständnis ist, daß sie auf die Abwesenheit eben dieser moralischen Qualität in einer bundesrepublikanischen Gesinnung verweist und eine banale Phrase beim Wort nimmt.

Schuldgeschichten der Dörfer

Neben ihrem essayistischen Werk sind es vor allem folgende Prosatexte, mit denen Herta Müller bekannt geworden ist: *Niederungen* (1982), *Der Mensch ist ein großer Fasan auf der Welt* (1986),

Barfüßiger Februar (1987), *Reisende auf einem Bein* (1989), *Der Fuchs war damals schon der Jäger* (1992), *Herztier* (1994) und *Heute wär ich mir lieber nicht begegnet* (1997). Ihre Literatur steht ein für die rumäniendeutsche Literatur (sog. fünfte deutsche Literatur), wie die Werke der Banater Schwaben und Siebenbürger Sachsen genannt werden, die in die Tradition von Paul Celan und Rose Ausländer gestellt werden. Dabei schreibt Herta Müller, wie andere rumäniendeutsche Autoren, Familienromane als Schuldgeschichten ihrer Dörfer. In der Vergangenheit dieser Dörfer gab es die Erfahrung von Nationalsozialismus und Krieg, in der Gegenwart die des kommunistischen Diktators. Sujet ihrer literarischen Darstellung ist also das Leben unter der Diktatur. Und so wie die totalitäre Macht sich in den Texten zur Sichtbarkeit verdichtet (so z.B. ein Hauptmann, der sein Opfer unter Zuhilfenahme seines Hundes sadistisch verhört), so gibt es auch eine Gegenbewegung im Text, die Bewegung des Individuums, das in seiner Angst widerständig gegen die Diktatur ist und das in dünne Fäden der Freundschaft eingewebt ist.

Ich möchte ein kurzes Textbeispiel geben, um zu zeigen, wie Herta Müller einen Zusammenhang von Poesie und Unterdrückung herstellt. In ihrem Roman *Herztier* beschreibt sie eine Verhörszene im Gefängnis – darin in gewisser Weise Tabucchis Roman *Erklärt Pereira* ähnlich:

> Der Hauptmann Pjele, der so hieß wie sein Hund, verhörte Edgar, Kurt und Georg das erste Mal wegen dieses Gedichts.
> Der Hauptmann Pjele hatte das Gedicht auf einem Blatt. Er zerknüllte das Blatt, der Hund Pjele bellte. Kurt mußte den Mund öffnen, und der Hauptmann stopfte ihm das Blatt hinein. Kurt mußte das Gedicht essen. Beim Essen mußte er würgen. Der Hund Pjele sprang ihn zweimal an. Er zerriß ihm die Hose und zerkratzte ihm die Beine. Beim dritten Sprung hätte der Hund Pjele bestimmt gebissen, meinte Kurt. Aber der Hauptmann Pjele sagte müde und ruhig: Pjele, es reicht. Der Hauptmann Pjele klagte über seine Nierenschmerzen und sagte: Du hast Glück mit mir. (*HT*, 87 f.)

Das Gedicht, um das es geht und das die Protagonistin versucht, im Verlauf der Handlung immer wieder auswendig aufzusagen, ist so harmlos wie schwerwiegend. Es lautet:

Jeder hatte einen Freund in jedem Stückchen Wolke
so ist das halt mit Freunden wo die Welt voll
   Schrecken ist
auch meine Mutter sagte das ist ganz normal
Freunde kommen nicht in Frage
denk an seriösere Dinge. (*HT*, 86)

Man muß diese sechs Gedichtzeilen mehrfach lesen, um am Ende die Grausamkeit des Securitate-Mannes, der das Gedicht als Aufforderung zur Flucht liest, zu erfassen, aber eben nicht zu verstehen. Es ist allein die Behauptung von Individualität, von Freundschaftsbanden, eben das Stückchen Wolke, das im Idiom eines Geheimdienstapparates nicht aufgeht. Und anders als in Tabucchis Roman geht es hier nicht um die innere Wandlung einer Figur, um die politische Läuterung, sondern die hier beschriebenen totalitären Strukturen sind zu stark, die Angst ist zu groß, die Sprachlosigkeit der Figuren zu dominierend, als daß ein universeller Widerstand beschrieben werden könnte. Das moralische Moment steckt im Detail und im lyrischen Ton.

Dabei benutzt Herta Müller immer wieder poetische Bilder, Metaphern und mythische Konstrukte, um die Details ihrer Heimat, aber auch ihrer Emigration zu zeigen. Herta Müller, die in Nitzkydorf/Kreis Timis in Rumänien geboren ist, gehört zur nationalen Minderheit der deutschsprachigen Banater Schwaben. Von 1972 bis 1976 studierte sie an der Universität von Temeswar Germanistik und Romänistik. Danach wurde sie immer wieder aus dem Schuldienst – sie arbeitete als Deutschlehrerin –, aber auch aus anderen Arbeitsstellen entfernt. Schließlich weigerte sie sich 1980, für den rumänischen Geheimdienst zu arbeiten. Aufgrund der großen Anerkennung, die ihr erster Prosaband *Niederungen* (1982) in der Bundesrepublik Deutschland fand, konnte sie zwar kurzfristig als Lehrerin wieder arbeiten, doch der politische Druck auf sie hielt an, so daß sie 1985 einen Ausreiseantrag stellte. Bis zur Genehmigung 1987 wurde sie in Rumänien mit einem strikten Reise- und Publikationsverbot belegt. Seit ihrer Ausreise 1987 lebt sie nun als freie Schriftstellerin in Berlin. Das Besondere an ihrer Schreibweise ist, daß sie anstelle psychologisierender Interpretationen von dem spricht, was gesagt wird, aber auch wie die Oberfläche ihrer Umgebung geschaffen ist und dabei die Dinge und Ereignisse nicht verdunkelt. Ihr Prosatext *Niederungen* steht ein – wie sie selbst sagt – für die Banat-Ebene, für eine Niederung, die noch tiefer als eine Ebene ist und im übertragenen Sinn für »das niedrige Bewußtsein, das Nicht-in-die-Höhe-blicken-Wollen und das Nicht-über-sich-hinausschauen-Können«.[11] Sie berichtet von der Rückständigkeit der dörflichen Enklave und zeichnet ein dörfliches Lebensgemälde mit schweren Beschädigungen. Eine Dorfchronik, die zum Fragment wird und nicht im erzählerischen Organismus aufgeht.[12] Eine Mikrowelt, die nicht unschuldig ist. Also keine Sentimentalität, kein Romantizismus, keine Idyllik, keine poetische Natur oder grün-alternative Wanderbewegung. Sondern ein Widerstand gegen die Provinzialität, d.h. gegen die Provinz und die ideologischen Beschränkungen des Heimatbegriffs. So auch in ihrem schon erwähnten Roman mit dem Titel *Herztier*, in dem sie den Ceauşescu-Sozialismus beschreibt: »Alle bleiben hier Dörfler. Wir sind mit dem Kopf von zu Hause weggegangen, aber mit den Füßen stehen wir in einem anderen Dorf. In einer Diktatur kann es keine Städte geben, weil alles klein ist, wenn es bewacht wird« (*HT*, 52).

Und doch bleibt etwas hängen, Details der Heimat als Erlebnisgrund in ihren Texten. In *Barfüßiger Februar* (1987) beschreibt sie den Weg ihrer Emigration nach Westberlin: »Was ist das für ein Land, das an den Fingern reißt, wenn man den Koffer hebt. Das man zwischen den Augen sieht, weit über dem Gehirn wie draußen überm Feld. [. . .] Was ist das für ein Gegenstand, der, wenn man ihn verlassen hat, wie eine Kugel wird« (*BF*, 49).

Das Unheimliche der Mythen

Ihre Rückgewinnung des Themas Heimat ist eine, die sich den ideologischen Besetzungen des Heimatbegriffs entgegenstellt und einen Begriff der Heimatlosigkeit dagegen setzt. Es ist ein Erzählen, das die Dorfgeschichte in ihren ideologischen Verkrustungen verabschiedet und im Archaischen und der Tradierung nationaler Mythen das Schreckliche erkennt. Herta Müllers Mythenkritik steht einer Anknüpfung an nationale mythische Traditionen entgegen, die heldisch aggressive Vorstellungen unterstützt. Damit sind ihre Texte in Kontrast zu lesen und widersprechen einer Bewegung, wie sie sich z.B. seit den 60er Jahren, vor allem aber in den 70er und 80er Jahren in der serbischen Literatur abzeichnete. Ich erwähne dies deshalb, weil Herta Müller sich entschieden gegen die serbisch-nationalistischen Aussagen gewandt hat und als Schriftstellerin – ganz im Gegensatz zu Handkes Intervention mit seinen beiden Büchern zu Serbien – politisch Stellung bezogen hat. Denn für sie »ersetzt« »die serbische Landkarte das Gewissen«, und es geht ihr darum, »die Wurzeln nationaler Propaganda« zu analysieren.[13] So existierte das Phänomen in der zeitgenössischen serbischen Literatur, daß das Wilde und Barbarische der Traditionen weitergeschrieben wurde – u.a. in der Verwendung des Wolfsmythos. Der lahme Wolf, verfolgt und geschunden, steht für das seiner nationalen Würde und Kraft beraubte Serbien. Ein Wolf, der aber wieder zu Kräften kommen wird und im Wolfsrudel – einer zusammengerotteten Horde – Rache nehmen wird. Diese Wolfsfigur – darauf verweist Reinhard Lauer – erfährt nun ihre Renaissance in der serbischen Literatur und wird ungebrochen weiter tradiert. Und er zitiert: »Die Wölfe werden kommen, werden kommen« – so in einem serbischen Gedicht von 1984.[14]

Und so wie der Wolf dämonisiert wurde, geschah ähnliches im Volksglauben vieler Kulturen mit dem Fuchs. Auf das Bild des verschlagenen Fuchses und die mythischen Geschichten um den Fuchs spielt Herta Müllers Roman *Der Fuchs war damals schon der Jäger* (1992) an. Das Bild des Fuchses wird aber hier gänzlich anders verwendet und nicht mythisch überfrachtet. Adina, die Hauptfigur des Buches, bekam als Kind vor zehn Jahren ein Fuchsfell geschenkt. Es gab ihr Wärme und Geborgenheit, sie nahm das weiche Fell in den immer schwieriger werdenden Zeiten als eine Art Talisman an. Jetzt lebt sie als Lehrerin in einer rumänischen Stadt. Als Adina von der Staatssicherheit observiert wird, benutzt der Machtapparat den Fuchs als Mittel im Nervenkrieg. Um sie einzuschüchtern, schneiden die Securitate-Offiziere bei ihren heimlichen Besuchen in ihrer Wohnung in wohlkalkulierten Abständen den Schwanz und schließlich die Füße des Fuchses ab. Das abgetrennte Teil legen sie dann so korrekt wieder an, daß eine Schnittstelle nicht erkennbar ist. Als Adina schließlich auf dem Fell ausrutscht, bemerkt sie die Veränderung. Nur zu gerne möchte sie zunächst glauben, der Schwanz sei von selbst abgefallen, aber der Geheimdienst hat auf infame Weise zugleich Spuren beseitigt und gelegt. So wirkt der scheinbar minimale Eingriff viel bedrohlicher, als roh verwüstete Räume es sein könnten. Herta Müllers poetisches Bild des Fuchses ist deutlich und artifiziell zugleich, jedoch nicht verschlüsselt, sondern es steht für sich selbst ein: »Zuerst ist der Schwanz abgetrennt, dann die Beine – und nach dem Sturz Ceauşescus wird der Kopf abgeschnitten.«[15]

Damit steht ihre Verwendung von mythischen Bildern und Metaphern aber auch im Gegensatz zu einer Semantik der Mythen, die gefährliche Potentiale der Militanz, des Nationalismus, der Grausamkeit und Intoleranz in sich bergen, die, wie auch die Entwicklung in Serbien und Bosnien zeigte, unmittelbar ins Leben treten können. Das Gewalttätige der Sitten in einer Diktatur kann also ohne weiteres im Gegensatz zur Sittlichkeit, zu den Normen des Guten stehen, und das Grauen ist häufig nichts anderes als eine Verlängerung der Volkssitten. Und wenn Humanität in der Literatur überhaupt einen Sinn hat, dann besteht diese in der Entdeckung, daß die Menschen in ihrer unmittelbar naturwüchsigen Bestimmtheit eben nicht aufgehen. Deshalb liegen die Begriffe Heimat und das Unheimliche bei Herta Müller so dicht beieinander.

Das lyrische Moment

Die Verlebendigung des moralischen Moments, die Auratisierung durch Metaphern, der Rhythmus, in dem Erinnerungen auftauchen, das Wechselspiel von Innenansicht der Protagonisten und Außenwelt und die lyrischen Passagen im Text bewahren ein *Geheimnis*, nämlich dort, wo die Überschreitung und die Positionierung des Subjekts beginnt. Georges-Arthur Goldschmidt hat darauf verwiesen, daß dies die deutsche Sprache sehr treffend sagt, »denn *heim* – in *Geheimnis, heimlich, verheimlichen* – enthält das zum Heim Gehörende, das Familiäre, das Intime. Weil meine Intimität intim ist, muß ich sie verbergen: Ich vereinige ja das Weltall in meiner Hand; mir es entwenden, hieße mich meiner selbst berauben.«[16] Aber es steckt in diesem Wort auch der Umschlag: das Unheimliche, das gerade auch aus der Heimat und dem Vertrauten hervorgeht.

Herta Müller hat in ihren Essays und in ihren Lehrveranstaltungen immer wieder auf die Bedeutung verwiesen, die Gedichte für das Überleben von Schriftstellern haben können. In einem Essay zu Ruth Klügers *weiter leben* (1992), in dem das Überleben in den Konzentrationslagern Theresienstadt und Auschwitz-Birkenau geschildert wird, schreibt Herta Müller, eng an Ruth Klügers Text argumentierend:

Wie Paul Celan so stellt auch Ruth Klüger fest: »Keine Sprache beherrschen als die der Verächter dieses Volkes, keine Gelegenheit haben,
eine andere zu lernen.« An dieser Sprache, die es vorher gab als sensi-
bles Wort, hielt sie sich fest, an den Fetzen der Balladen, unverständ-
lich für ein Kind. Dennoch ließen sie sich aufsagen im Kopf. Und sie
gaben den Füßen die Kraft, stundenlang reglos im Hof bei den Appel-
len zu stehen: »Die Schillerschen Balladen wurden dann auch meine
Appellgedichte.« Ihr »scheint es indessen, daß der Inhalt der Verse erst
in zweiter Linie von Bedeutung war und daß uns in erster Linie die
Form selbst, die gebundene Sprache, eine Stütze gab. Oder vielleicht
ist auch diese schlichte Deutung schon zu hoch gegriffen, und man
sollte zu allererst feststellen, daß Verse, indem sie die Zeit einteilen, im
wörtlichen Sinne ein Zeitvertreib sind.« Dann schrieb die Überlebende
selber Gedichte, um sich auszuhalten: »[. . .] da wollte ich mein Er-
lebnis verarbeiten, auf die einzige Weise, die ich kannte, in ordentli-
chen, gegliederten Gedichtstrophen.« (*FA*, 37 f.)

Gedichte also als Gegengewicht zum Chaos, als lebendiger Rhythmus in einer schrecklichen und grausamen Wirklichkeit. Die lyrische Form als Rettungsanker im Konzentrationslager. So hat es
Ruth Klüger berichtet, ähnlich auch Jorge Semprun in *Schreiben
oder Leben* (1995), wenn er davon spricht, wie er in Buchenwald,
zusammen mit seinen Mitgefangenen, Verse von Heinrich Heine
deklamiert habe:

> Ich weiß nicht, was soll es bedeuten,
> Daß ich so traurig bin [. . .][17]

Das Gebet, das Kaddisch, aber auch Gedichte gliedern die Zeit,
produzieren Sinn oder Unsinn – allein durch den Rhythmus der
Sprache, durch die Farbigkeit und Vieldeutigkeit der benutzten
Bilder. Herta Müller hat das Potential, das in gereimten Versen
steckt, erkannt. Auch wenn sie davon berichtet, wie sie – damals
noch in Rumänien in Zeiten der Ceauşescu-Diktatur und der Zeit
ihrer Verfolgung durch die Securitate – auf dem Weg zu Freunden
oder westdeutschen Verlegern ihre verbotenen Prosatexte eng am
Körper trug und dabei zu ihrer eigenen Beruhigung ihr bekannte
und geläufige Gedichte aufsagte. Jeder Schritt und jedes Wort
bildeten so eine Art Geheimpakt gegen die lähmende Angst. Insofern ist es vielleicht auch kein Zufall, wenn – wie in zahlreichen
Rezensionen – immer wieder vom lyrischen Ton innerhalb ihrer
Prosa gesprochen wird.

Zugleich hat sie mit diesem Verständnis, nämlich das Lyrische als Moment des Widerstands zu verstehen, ein Gegengewicht geschaffen zu der Vorstellung des Gedichts als Hymne oder Besingen schrecklicher Taten – wie es gerade ja im nationalistischen Gedankengut üblich ist. In seinem letzten Prosatext, den Joseph Brodsky im Dezember 1995, vier Wochen vor seinem Tod, verfaßt hat, geht es um den Zusammenhang von Gefangenschaft und Offenbarung, Leben und Literatur. Dieser Text ist als Vorwort zu dem Buch *This Prison Where I Live* erschienen. Danach gehört das Gefängnis für Schriftsteller im zwanzigsten Jahrhundert fast zum Berufsbild. Die eigene Metaphysik, die eigenen moralischen Vorstellungen schrumpfen unter dem Apparat von Unterdrückung und Zwang auf die bündigsten Formulierungen, auf kompakte Ausdrucksweisen, auf das, was man reproduzieren kann. Um ein bißchen Licht ins Dunkel zu bringen, so Brodsky: »[. . .] müssen Sie Reim und Metrum verwenden: damit Sie sich das Zeug merken können, vor allem im Hinblick auf manche Verhörmethoden, die oft die Zuverlässigkeit Ihres Hinterkopfes beeinträchtigen.« Das Schreiben gebundener Lyrik, das Dichten im Kopf ist neben Liegestützen und kalten Waschungen eine Möglichkeit der Selbstbewahrung. Darüber hinaus wohnt nach Brodsky gerade dem Lyrischen etwas Besonderes inne: »[. . .] daß das Wesen jedes guten Gedichts Verdichtung und Schnelligkeit ist«. Die lyrische gebundene Form *erhebt* in einem gewissen Sinne – auch über Stacheldraht und Gefängnismauern hinweg. Die Folge ist für Brodsky, der ja selber 1964 als »arbeitsscheuer Parasit« zur Zwangsarbeit in einem russischen Lager verurteilt war, »daß es fesselndere Dinge gibt als die Zerbrechlichkeit des eigenen Körpers oder den Todeskampf der eigenen Seele«.[18]

Herta Müller hat kürzlich in einer von ihr verfaßten Rezension zu einem Buch über Paul Celan vom Gedichtesprechen gesprochen, von der jüdischen, russischen, rumänischen langen Tradition, von dem »rhythmisch singenden Ton, der durch den ganzen Körper läuft«. Und sie hat erwähnt, wie Celan während einer Lesung vor der Gruppe 47 von vielen schnell und kaum gewendeten Deutschen für seine Art des Vorlesens geradezu ausgelacht wurde. »Daß sie nichts begreifen von einer deutschen Sprache, in der Wortspiele ›Zungenspäße‹ genannt werden«.[19]

Herta Müllers Leistung ist es zu zeigen, wie repressive Strukturen tradiert werden, wie kollektive Normen, das Niederschmetternde und Unterdrückende des allgemeinen Gesetzes im

Gegensatz zu dem Humanen stehen können. Deshalb versucht sie, den Terror in seinen subtilen Facetten im totalitären System der Ceauşescu-Zeit zu schildern, zu demonstrieren, wie die Diktatur Menschen beschädigt, aber auch wie Menschen Widerstand leisten. Die Frage also nach dem richtigen Handeln ist im Zungenschlag dagegen, im poetischen Ton, aber auch in der Gestaltung ihrer Bilder und Metaphern zu finden. Darin behauptet sie den Platz der Moral innerhalb der Literatur.

Anmerkungen

[1] Vgl. Theodor W. Adorno, *Probleme der Moralphilosophie* (Frankfurt am Main, Suhrkamp, 1996), 19.

[2] Vgl. Tzvetan Todorov, *Angesichts des Äußersten* (München, Fink, 1993) (1991), 37.

[3] Ebd., 40; Todorov zit. Levi.

[4] Vgl. ebd., 42.

[5] Ebd., 47; Todorov zit. Semprun.

[6] Vgl. ebd., 19.

[7] Vgl. Adorno, *Probleme der Moralphilosophie*, 23.

[8] Ebd., 38; Adorno zit. Kant.

[9] Vgl. u.a. ihren Essayband *In der Falle* (Göttingen, Wallstein, 1996) oder aber auch eine Rezension wie 'Zungenspäße und Büßerschnee. Wie Helmut Böttiger mich durch "Orte Paul Celans" führte', *Die Zeit*, 6 Dezember 1996, 3.

[10] Herta Müller, 'Wahrheit danach. Warum wir aus Diktaturen nichts lernen', *Frankfurter Allgemeine Zeitung*, 4 Mai 1995.

[11] '"Mir scheint jede Umgebung lebensfeindlich". Ein Gespräch mit der rumäniendeutschen Schriftstellerin Herta Müller', *Süddeutsche Zeitung*, 16 November 1984.

[12] Sibylle Cramer, 'Provinz als mentaler Zustand', *Frankfurter Rundschau*, 7 Oktober 1987.

[13] Vgl. 'Die Tage werden weitergehen. Nur eine militärische Intervention könnte die serbische Aggression stoppen' (*HS*, 157–63); und 'Auf die Gedanken fällt Erde' (*HS*, 164–71).

[14] Reinhard Lauer, 'Aus Mördern werden Helden', *Frankfurter Allgemeine Zeitung*, 6 März 1993.

[15] Interview, Martin Doerry und Volker Hage, '"So eisig, kalt und widerlich". Die Schriftstellerin Herta Müller über eine Aktion deutscher Autoren gegen den Fremdenhaß', *Der Spiegel*, 9 November 1992, 264–8.

[16] Georges-Arthur Goldschmidt, *Der bestrafte Narziß* (Zürich, Ammann, 1994), 62.

[17] Vgl. Jorge Semprun, *Schreiben oder Leben* (Frankfurt am Main, Suhrkamp, 1995), 54 f.

[18] Joseph Brodsky, 'Ein Sonnensystem von sechzig Watt', *Frankfurter Allgemeine Zeitung*, 15 Januar 1997.

[19] Müller, 'Zungenspäße und Büßerschnee', 3.

9

'Leben wir im Detail': Herta Müller's Micro-Politics of Resistance

BRIGID HAINES

> They knew that there was nowhere for them to go. They had nothing.
> No future. So they stuck to the small things.
> Arundhati Roy, *The God of Small Things*

Arundhati Roy's bestselling novel *The God of Small Things* tells the story of what cannot be: a love affair between a married woman from a middle-class Anglo-Indian Syrian Christian family and a member of the untouchable caste, the Paravans. Aware that their love breaks every taboo and can have no existence in the rigidly stratified society of modern India (it ends, predictably, in violence and enduring tragedy), the couple resist in the only way open to them, namely by creating a temporary private space and taking delight in the details of the moment. Herta Müller's texts, though the product of a very different world, also document and are documents of the seemingly impossible, namely of resistance to inhuman and deadly social and political orders, a resistance practised by means of attending stubbornly to the particular, the individual, the local, the detail. The focus on detail which, as will be demonstrated below, originated for Müller as both an aesthetic strategy and a basic survival mechanism in the face of the life-denying master plots of totalitarianism, is an abiding feature of her politics and her aesthetics, and provides a crucial link between her essays and her literary works. As a politics, the highlighting of the particular, with its concomitant relinquishing of attempts to project a wider picture, is problematic, for it appears to offer stasis rather than a way forward, opposition to what is, rather than proposals for what might be, and a subjective, unstable, non-aligned opposition at that; yet, unlike Roy's, Müller's is ultimately not a tragic world but one in which the individual survives against all the odds, and in the heterogeneous, postmodern era this offers liberating possibilities. As an aesthetics the focus on detail has a more complex result, leading as it does to the building up of new aesthetic patterns and a degree of artistic control, while at the same time involving the reader in the creation of subjective meanings, thus taking care not to impose hermeneutic closure.

Müller's essays wear their resistance openly. They are polemical, self-assured, and rooted in personal experience; they frequently, with more or less excellent justification, have an underlying moral message. Many consist of angry exposés of abuses of power that the author has experienced at first or second hand, for example in the Nazi period, in her native Romania under the Ceauşescu regime, in contemporary Germany, or in other parts of the world, for example the former Yugoslavia. Some of the essays in the volume *Hunger und Seide*, for example, recount in vivid, often absurd, and sometimes gruesome detail many of the appalling degradations of life in Ceauşescu's Romania. Müller also in this volume analyses the linguistic and ideological structures by means of which totalitarian regimes generally terrorize their citizens, comments on injustices in contemporary Germany, such as the treatment of asylum seekers and the failure of German politicians to counter racism, and urges her readers to recognize the problem posed by Serbian aggression in the Balkans. The essays in the volume *In der Falle* look back to celebrate the lives of three writers who all were or have been victims in some way of political oppression, and the integrity of whose work has inspired Müller, namely Theodor Kramer, the First World War Austrian Jewish poet who escaped the Holocaust only to languish in the misery of exile; Inge Müller, the poet, who lived though the Second World War, co-wrote some of the plays of her husband, Heiner Müller, and committed suicide in 1966, tortured by a sense of complicity in the crimes of German history; and Ruth Klüger, an Ausschwitz survivor whose harrowing account of her life, *weiter leben*, has recently been published to critical acclaim.[1] In two more recent essays published in newspapers Müller is outspoken in her criticism of Helmut Kohl, and in her defence of the Iranian writer accused of spying, Faradsch Sarkuhi.[2] (She has also taken a public stand against the bringing together of the East and West German PEN clubs and on the controversy surrounding the scientist Annemarie Schimmel, and joined in the criticism of the East German writer Sascha Anderson for his *Stasi* links.)[3] Linked by a prevailing tone of indignation, Müller's essays thus chart abuses of human rights, remember the victims, champion those who have had the courage to resist, condemn collaborators, and urge the reader not to shy away from difficult moral judgements. On the subject of the *Stasi* debate, for example, she states unequivocally that, 'Man muß in keiner Diktatur gelebt haben, um über sie zu urteilen' (*HS*, 29). While these essays make compelling reading, the suspicion that Müller's moral certainty, acquired, admittedly, under conditions where the wrongs were awfully clear, sometimes leads her into hasty assessments and a levelling out of nuances[4] is confirmed when, in *In der Falle*, she goes so far as to offer a typology of four possible ways in which those caught up in dictatorships can react, ranging from voluntary collaboration, via collaboration under pressure, through non-collaboration because the need does not arise (these people become 'Mitläufer'), to the only position with which, one strongly suspects, she sympathizes, namely outright opposition (*FA*, 11–16). It is of course worth remembering here that Müller herself lost her job and presented herself as a target for draconian political repression for refusing to collaborate with the *Securitate*; she thus speaks with the authority of one who did resist in a perilous situation where there was no organized opposition to defend her, and, unlike many of Ceauşescu's victims, lived to tell the tale. Nevertheless, though she states that those who have lived under totalitarian rule are broken by the experience – 'Überlebende sind Zerbrochene' (*FA*, 36) – the implication of the simple typology above is that an inner core of the individual will always remain inviolate and should thus be capable of the resistance which she perceives to be a moral duty. This is, as one reviewer has pointed out, a utopian position, for 'Vielleicht gibt es kein "Menschenrecht auf Feigheit", wie Heiner Müller überspitzt sagte. Aber die Feigheit wird auch nicht durch ein moralisches Verdikt aus der Welt geschafft werden. Wer das verlangt, denkt nicht unbedingt human, sondern eher – utopisch'.[5]

The charge of utopian thinking is, ironically, the one above all others which Müller would most vigorously reject, for reasons which will become apparent. It is less easily applied to her literary works, which are more abstract, differentiated, and controlled, and offer a more complex view of the human subject's capacity to resist, as well as a more frightening, because more psychological, depiction of the state's ability to control individuals' lives through terror. Like the essays, they also mirror in their subject matter the trajectory of the author's life, which has been characterized by resistance: to the stifling norms of the Banat-Swabian village in which she grew up, to the intrusive and deadly power of the Romanian dictatorship which repressed Müller and her friends in the *Aktionsgruppe Banat*, to the rigid bureaucrats in the West German *Bundesnachrichtendienst* who, on her arrival in West Berlin in 1987, could not accept that she was both an ethnic German *and* a political refugee (*HS*, 25; *RB*, 26 ff.). Most of her literary works, which she likes to describe using the term 'autofiktional', feature a central female character who bears a close relationship with the author at various stages in her life: the 'Ich' in *Niederungen* (1982), who observes, fears, but does not always comprehend the restrictions and cruelties of village life from her child's perspective; Adine, in *Der Fuchs war damals schon der Jäger* (1992), a teacher subjected to systematic psychological terror by the Romanian security forces; the 'Ich' in *Herztier* (1994), one of a group of intellectuals targeted by the same security forces for special repression; the 'Ich' in *Heute wär ich mir lieber nicht begegnet* (1997), a factory worker who is summoned for daily interrogations as a punishment for wanting to leave the country; and Irene, in *Reisende auf einem Bein* (1989), who, having left the totalitarian state behind, describes her sense of disorientation on arrival in the Western city.

Like Müller herself, the protagonists are survivors, though their friends, like Müller's, often perish, the most poignant example being the figure of Georg in *Herztier*, based on the poet Rolf Bossert, who committed suicide in Frankfurt in February 1986.[6] While they owe their survival in part to luck (in particular Adine, whose escape from Romania is only made possible by the unexpected fall of the Ceaușescu regime), and it is left open whether the 'Ich' in *Heute wär ich mir lieber nicht begegnet* survives at all, they also resist in small ways the pressures to which they are subject, and thus retain their sanity and integrity: the 'Ich' in *Niederungen* sublimates her silent opposition into frenzied dreams; Adine rejects her friend Clara because of her affair with an officer of the *Securitate* and refuses to collaborate herself; the friends in *Herztier* find strength in their mutual support, and through keeping their friendship alive even after the state separates them physically, although ultimately the burdens placed on their friendship prove intolerable; Irene refuses to let her asylum case be processed according to the prescribed system of the West German authorities. Sometimes resistance is practised through taking the long view of oppression, for example the comment in *Der Fuchs war damals schon der Jäger* that cockroaches will survive socialism (*FJ*, 114); alternatively it can take the form of perpetuating folk songs and traditions held by the authorities to be subversive (as the Hauptmann Pjele, the interrogator in *Herztier*, says, 'Das bürgerlich-gutsherrliche Regime ist längst überwunden. Heute singt unser Volk andere Lieder', *HT*, 89). In extreme cases it means a defiant refusal to commit suicide: 'So dumm war ich und vertrieb mit dem Lachen das Weinen. So stur, daß ich mir dachte: Der Fluß ist nicht mein Sack. Dich stecken wir ins Wasser gelingt dem Hauptmann Pjele nicht' (*HT*, 112).

The resistance here arises out of a kind of instinctual stubbornness,[7] and has been described by Müller as beginning not as a political,

> sondern eine *moralische* Geste [. . .]: instinktives Ausscheren aus Überdruß am Ticken der Norm. [. . .] Je eigentlicher, je zuverläßiger Widerstand war, um so mehr war er nichts weiter als eine moralische Geste. Er begann im eigenen Schädel, im Alleinsein vor seinem eigenen Bild. Er kam aus dem Festhalten an moralischen Vorstellungen von sich selbst. Aus dem Bedürfnis, trotz aller lebenslästiger Konsequenzen anständig zu bleiben. (*HS*, 91 f.)

Paradoxically she goes on to claim that opposition originated for her not in courage but in 'Angst', for 'nur sie macht eigenwillig und stur' (*HS*, 92). All of this suggests a softer, more subjective view of morality than that implied in the essays referred to above, one in which, as Norbert Otto Eke has recently argued, morality has been uncoupled from Kantian 'Verstand', and is thus vulnerable, isolated, and no longer underwritten by a regard for the common good or the process of history.[8] It has become, in fact, definitively private, originating 'wo niemand außer einem selber hinsieht – bei der kleinsten Geste. Wenn es etwas *Privates* gibt, dann ist es die Moral' (*FA*, 27 f.).

Such opposition is also bought at a heavy cost: neither Müller nor her protagonists survive unscathed. Müller's continued preoccupation with bearing witness to the 'Angst' which is a condition of life for those living under totalitarianism is evident in the choice of subject matter of her most recent novels: *Reisende auf einem Bein*, the text in which she appeared to have left the theme of dictatorship behind and be turning her attention to the different

structures of life in the West in order to explore the ambivalent
freedoms conferred on the city dweller under capitalism, appeared
in 1989, but was then followed by her bleakest depictions yet of
the mutilating effects of political repression in Romania in the
trilogy *Der Fuchs war damals schon der Jäger* (1992), *Herztier* (1994),
and *Heute wär ich mir lieber nicht begegnet* (1997). She has not
paused to revel in the power which, according to Elias Canetti, is
felt by survivors of oppression: 'Der Augenblick des *Überlebens* ist
der Augenblick der Macht'.[9] Indeed, in a recent *Guardian* interview
she described her reaction to Ceauşescu's death at Christmas 1989
in terms not of empowerment, but of sadness: 'For 15 years I wished him dead every day. I thought that when he was executed I'd
be so relieved. But I had the opposite reaction. I couldn't stop
weeping. I found it hard to watch a man being shot. And he was
a man for the first time. He was unshaven, he had this fear in his
eyes'.[10] Rather, the more time passes since the downfall of the
particular regime which she knew so intimately, the more urgent
for Müller becomes the task of writing about totalitarianism, and
the more overwhelming her estimation of its power, for while
both *Der Fuchs war damals schon der Jäger* and *Herztier* end with
escape to the West, *Heute wär ich mir lieber nicht begegnet*, analysed
in detail below, offers less in the way of hope.

The lasting effects of oppression are felt by her protagonists too:
of the five friends of the central character in *Herztier*, for example,
four are dead by the end of the novel, and she and the other
survivor, Edgar, are burdened by the futile attempt to make sense
of their deaths. Looking back on their behaviour they can discern
no correct course of action, for the regime left them none: 'Wenn
wir schweigen, werden wir unangenehm, [. . .] wenn wir reden,
werden wir lächerlich. [. . .] wir [waren] für uns selber ein
Fehler' (*HT*, 7). Irene too is at first unable to take advantage of the
multiple new identities offered to her by life in the Western city
because she has grown used to defining herself in relation to the
contours of the life she left behind. She perceives the *Bundesnachrichtendienst* official who interviews her as essentially no different
from the state security men in 'das andere Land' that she has left
behind, and though it leads in the main to disappointment and
rejection, she repeatedly seeks out emotional intimacy as a means
of self-definition. Like the man in Paul's anecdote who survives an
accident where an axe becomes lodged in his brain, only to die
when doctors remove it (*FJ*, 108 f.), it seems at first possible that

she will paradoxically not survive the removal from a life-threatening situation. However, unlike Edgar and the 'Ich' in *Herztier*, she focuses on the details of the present rather than dwelling on the past, not attempting to make sense of what she sees, but rather, in her experiments with collage, maximizing chance and contingency. As Margaret Littler has demonstrated in her contribution to this volume, Irene's deliberate short-sightedness and renunciation of understanding when faced with the infinitely plural sense impressions offered to her by the Western city become a liberating opportunity, and she learns to adapt well enough to survive.

Resistance is for Müller more than a set of actions. While she insists on the importance of personal experience as a basis for her work, and, for example, cherishes the writings of Ruth Klüger, Inge Müller and Theodor Kramer because they are 'nicht bloß *Literatur* [. . .]. Sie sind mehr als das, weil gleichzeitig Beweis für die persönliche Integrität schreibender Personen' (*FA*, 6), her auto-fiction is, of course, not only autobiographically based, but also *fiction*, and as such offers resistance through its aesthetic patterning and focus on detail. To understand fully why the focus on detail is so central to both the content and the form of Müller's works it is necessary to look at the poetological essays in the volume *Der Teufel sitzt im Spiegel. Wie Wahrnehmung sich erfindet.* Müller has always been implacably opposed to the master narratives of totalitarianism, with their life-denying misuse of the concepts of utopia, freedom, and progress, and to their literary expression in socialist realism. Her experience of the fascist legacy and of life under Ceauşescu taught her that:

> Diese in die Realität umgesetzten Utopien sind immer ein Unglück geworden. Sie haben immer eine Diktatur ergeben. Für mich ist das völlig logisch. Wenn eine Idee über alles Bescheid weiß, kann sie ja nichts anderes tun, als den Einzelnen nötigen und zwingen. Der neue Mensch, der im Sozialismus geschaffen werden sollte, war ein Monstrum. Das Ich war nicht ein Bestandteil des Wir, sondern immer der Feind des Wir. Individualismus war das schlimmste Wort.[11]

Dictatorship was for her an extension of the restrictive and stifling norms of the Swabian village in which she grew up: 'Die erste Diktatur, die ich kannte, war das banatschwäbische Dorf'.[12] Her strategy as a child was to combine her quite natural need to belong to the community with her simultaneous rejection of its norms through daily deception: 'Meine größte Arbeit war, das, was im Kopf stand, zu verstecken. Das Täuschen war die Arbeit meiner Kindheit' (*TS*, 13). From the close observation of details of daily life as seen through the eyes of a child in *Niederungen*, which allowed a wide-eyed laying bare of and simultaneous resistance to oppressive power structures, Müller developed her personal poetic and political manifesto, encapsulated in an exhortation borrowed from Ionesco, 'Leben wir also. Aber man läßt uns nicht leben. Leben wir also im Detail' (*HS*, 61). Living in the detail involves two political realizations, one practical and one theoretical: the individual being targeted for political repression cannot rely on any alliance whatsoever, ultimately not even that with close friends, for 'jede persönliche Nähe ist dem, was der Staat im Sinn hat und tut, nicht gewachsen',[13] but must survive on his or her own wits from moment to moment. He or she also cannot presume to project any future state of affairs where the individual would not be oppressed, because of the belief that all systems are by their very nature oppressive to someone, so must concentrate instead on the local. Similarly Müller's aesthetic resistance takes the form of focusing on observed and imagined detail (hence her favoured term 'die *erfundene* Wahrnehmnung', *TS*, 9–31 [my italics]), rather than than on plots and meanings, and thus evading the building of narratives for making sense of the world, with their inevitably prescriptive effects. Müller's implacable opposition to systems and theories of all kinds thus leads to her investment of significance in the detached detail, a significance which, in large part, she leaves to the reader to interpret.[14] In aesthetic terms this means playing with surprising, surreal juxtapositions, seen most clearly in her collages in the volume *Der Wächter nimmt seinen Kamm*, and in Irene's seemingly endless observations of unconnected details of Berlin life in *Reisende auf einem Bein*. It also means making use of the non-correspondence of meaning between the German language and Müller's other language, Romanian, of whose images she is very fond,[15] this latter strategy leading to a kind of linguistic drift. Though it may involve modifying them, this approach does not, however, mean doing without some of the basic novelistic ordering conventions, such as chronology, point of view, or poetic patterning. Indeed one of the most characteristic of Müller's narrative strategies is to invest observed, remembered or invented details with metonymic significance and repeat them,[16] thus creating homologizing metaphorical patterns which, as Ricarda Schmidt has argued in the case of *Herztier*, can serve to narrow down, rather than open up meanings.[17] Other critics, notably Norbert Otto Eke and Stephan Düppe, who both make much of her use of collage, have argued, however, that her novelistic prose works on the difference, allowing the reader creative space:[18] 'Schreiben wird [. . .] zum Versuch, einen Ort im Jenseits der Macht zu behaupten'.[19]

The tension highlighted here between Müller's anti-systematic poetics and the contradictory imposition of ordering structures is nowhere more clearly demonstrated than in the 'Herztier' motif in the novel of the same name. An invented formulation which Müller refuses to define ('Ich wollte dieses Wort ausbalancieren, daß es immer woandershin schillert'),[20] the term could be interpreted as supporting a basically humanist theory of the human subject, namely that human beings have in common their uniqueness as individuals: Ceauşescu's essential being is parasitic and ugly (he is nourished by the blood of his people, *HT*, 70), the narrator's is stubbornly, instinctually resistant (it is her 'Herztier' that saves her from suicide, *HT*, 111). On the other hand this poetic motif can be seen to support a materialist, changing, and thus non-essential deconstruction of subjectivity in that, rather than possessing an essence, individuals identify with learned subject positions, for example the narrator's 'Herztier' is Swabian (*HT*, 89), and the malevolent grandmother dominates the husband she has stolen from another woman by ridiculing his masculinity and making him believe in her negative image of him: 'Er liebt sie nicht, aber sie kann ihn beherrschen, indem sie zu ihm sagt: Dein Herztier ist eine Maus' (*HT*, 81). On another occasion, when the friends are about to be forcibly separated by the state, their 'Herztiere' disperse, anticipating the physical dispersal: 'Unsere Herztiere flohen wie Mäuse. Sie warfen das Fell hinter sich ab und verschwanden im Nichts. Wenn wir kurz nacheinander viel redeten, blieben sie länger in der Luft' (*HT*, 89 f.). Ricarda Schmidt reads this use of the 'Herztier' motif as indicative of the weakness of the friends' 'Lebenskraft' at this point, and it is clear that it marks a low point in their collective mood.[21] Since, however, the passage is immediately followed by their discussion of the letter-writing code with which they intend to deceive the authorities and keep real communication open, it is possible also to read the elusiveness of the 'Mäuse' in a more positive way as symbolic of

the friends' desire to elude the authorities. In examples like this
the author, whose presence often seems so dominant in the subject
matter and characteristic style of her works, achieves her aim of
disappearing behind the textuality of her writing, which becomes,
in a positive sense, groundless:

> Die erfundene Wahrnehmung hebt sich von der Wahrnehmung nicht
> ab. Sie geht eine Schicht darunter. Die erfundene Wahrnehmung ist
> das lückenlose Einsinken in die Wahrnehmung. Es entsteht ein doppel-
> ter, dreifacher, vielfacher Boden, der keiner ist. Vielleicht wie das Ge-
> fühl des Fadens, das Gefühl des Bodens. Dieses Vielfache des Bodens
> unter den Gedanken ist nicht Boden unter den Füßen. Es macht nicht
> sicher, es fängt nicht auf. (*TS*, 40)

A reader new to Müller would find her latest novel, *Heute wär
ich mir lieber nicht begegnet*, a more straightforward introduction to
her *œuvre* than any of the three novels which preceded it. It is con-
ventionally structured around the events of one morning as the
central character, again unnamed, but loosely modelled on Müller
herself,[22] takes a tram on her way to her regular interrogation, the
description of the journey being punctuated by flashbacks as she
reviews her life and remembers the events which led her to this
point. She does not reach her destination, and the denouement of
the last few pages undermines the basis on which she has found
the courage to resist when she discovers that her beloved, if
drunken, husband Paul, on whom she depends as her only ally
against the power of the state, has been spying on her. We do not
discover what happens to her; the text ends with her renewing
(despairingly?) her resolve not to allow the state to destroy her
sanity: 'Ha, ha, nicht irr werden' (*HB*, 240). The dramatic structure,
with its strong forward momentum and final undermining twist,
is very different from the episodic, though also basically chro-
nological, *Herztier*, with its strong poetic and metonymic patterning. The new novel also contains a great deal of local colour that
is reminiscent of Müller's earlier prose works about Romania,
Niederungen and *Barfüßiger Februar*, and the essays in *Hunger und
Seide*. We read, for example, of the layers of history impacting on
the present when the narrator unwittingly marries the son of the
man responsible for the forced deportation of her grandparents,
and hear in detail of the material and emotional hardships of
everyday life. In this sense it is less of a 'palimpsest of the

political'[23] than her other novels and more of a direct depiction of it, and requires less background knowledge of the history of and conditions prevailing in Romania to facilitate its understanding. This does not make it less effective. Of all Müller's novels it illustrates most strongly the power of the state to invade the private sphere and the near impossibility but absolute necessity of offering resistance. The individual is more than ever alone, more than ever penetrated in all aspects of her being by power, and more than ever unwilling to privilege her own 'Verstand' as the superior instrument with which to understand and combat what is happening to her, relying instead on instinctual resistance. She is in many ways a weak person who is led by her desires, living in the shadow of the older brother who died when still a baby (*HB*, 83), desiring her father because of an unresolved Electra complex (*HB*, 83), taking her identity from the clothes she wears (*HB*, 49), sleeping with the boss she dislikes because he suggests it and 'Ich hatte nichts dagegen' (*HB*, 177), and then, as a reaction to this and the interrogations which have just started, moving in with Paul on impulse two days after she meets him (*HB*, 60). Her explanation of this last act demonstrates once again that for Müller, defensive behaviour is instinctual and not dictated by 'Verstand': 'Ich redete mir alle Männer aus. Gerade dann blieb ich hängen an Paul, als ich auf Abwehr stand. Ich glaub, bei mir gleicht die Abwehr dem Verlangen, mehr als die Suche. So muß es gewesen sein, deshalb krallte ich mich an' (*HB*, 60).

The narrator's need for self-defence is extreme: in *Hunger und Seide* Müller recounted a childhood memory of a 'Doktorbuch', a kind of household medical textbook, which contained a model of a human body with numbered parts in the head and body cavities. Try as she might, after unpacking them she could never get the profusion of organs back into their correct position. She comments:

Jahre später, als ich die Geschädigten und Zerbrochenen im Lande sah, als ich von stundenlangen Verhören ohne Halt wie betrunken zwischen den Bäumen des Parks wieder nach Hause ging und mir jede Frage und meine Antwort darauf wieder und wieder durch den Kopf gehen ließ, als der Wind in den Bäumen zu groß war, und das Knakken der Äste wie Schritte hinter mir, als ich mich um den Preis des Schädelzerspringens von außen sehen wollte, um zu wissen, wo ich richtig und wo ich fasch reagiert hatte bei diesen vielen Fragen, spürte ich, daß mir die Schädeldecke offenstand. Mein Kopf war von fremden

Fingern durchwühlt. Damals fiel mir das Doktorbuch ein. Die
Securitate-Offiziere, die Wächter des Diktators hatten mit mir das gleiche getan, was ich mit dem Menschen im Doktorbuch getan hatte. (*HS*,
97)

Heute wär ich mir lieber nicht begegnet illustrates this process of the
invasion of the narrator's mind by the powers that be, and her
attempts to resist. The 'crime' for which she is being punished is
that of placing notes, on which the words 'Ti aspetto' and her
name and address are written, inside clothing bound for Italy in
the hope of finding an Italian husband and being able to leave the
country. This expression of desire is seen as dangerously subversive, and thereafter she is summoned for regular interrogations.
Her interrogator, Major Albu, seeks to inspire fear in her through
suspense ('Warum die Nerven verlieren, wir fangen erst an', *HB*,
11), sexual insults,[24] and the indirect threat of violence, the most
chilling moment being when he plants on her a box containing an
amputated human finger, an event to which he never subsequently refers. Despite the immense pressure which threatens to define
her totally ('Weil ich nichts bin, außer bestellt', *HB*, 54), she retains
her sanity through various means, ranging from the meticulous
observation of superstitious rituals in order to bring her luck (for
example always wearing the same blouse when she is going to be
interrogated), to making fun of the spy resident in her block by
buying him a notebook for his reports (*HB*, 221 f.), to more fool-
hardy acts such as approaching and starting an argument with the
spies observing her block from the outside (*HB*, 112 f.), and talk-
ing back to Major Albu, for example when she asks him 'Was
nehme ich dem Land, wenn ich in ein anderes gehe' (*HB*, 156),
and, in her last interrogation, asking him to replace the hair he has
removed from her shoulder because it belongs to her (*HB*, 227).
This incident meets with an unexpected reaction from Major Albu,
who laughs.[25] These instinctual acts of resistance help the narrator
to remain sane, but not necessarily intact. In order to resist she
compartmentalizes her life into what she labels 'das Glück', that is,
the private, deeply happy part of her life spent with her husband
Paul, which she leaves behind when she goes to be interrogated
(*HB*, 22, 29, 54 f.), and the rest. Her very thoughts are, however,
invaded and the place reserved for 'das Glück' threatened; to
counteract this she imagines filling her head with welcome and
unwelcome people and objects to replace the uncontrollable

thoughts about them which are plaguing her. In this way, some order could be restored:

> Es gäbe eine Ordnung: Mitten im Kopf steht Paul [. . .] Im Hinter-
> kopf, das läßt sich nicht vermeiden, im Hinterkopf ist Albus Laufbur-
> sche, der womöglich in dem roten Auto unten sitzt, bevor er hier läu-
> tet und mich bestellt. [. . .] Ja, lieber wär der Laufbursche persönlich
> in meinem Hinterkopf, statt seiner leisen Stimme, die sich einfrißt
> [. . .] Lauter feste Sachen, die im Kopf nur den Platz brauchen, auf
> dem sie stehen. Flächen und Kanten, die man sich in Halt und Last
> einteilen und ohne Mühe voneinander unterscheiden kann. Und in den
> Zwischenräumen bleibt Platz für das Glück. (*HB*, 110 f.)

This instinct to divide helps her again when, at the moment of great shock on discovering the human finger, she remains in control by dividing herself into the stressed self whose actions (in this case eating) are governed by a compulsive reaction to fear, and the detached, observing self: 'Ich war ja gesund, und den Kuchen aß eine Hinfällige, sie glaubte, essen zu müssen und aß um ihr Leben' (*HB*, 160). But dividing can only be taken so far. She cannot divide thoughts from feelings, she refuses to attempt to comprehend (and thus become complicit in the horrors of) a reality she senses to be wrong:

> Manche Leute trennen nicht nur Gegenstände von Gedanken, sie tren-
> nen auch Gedanken von Gefühlen. Ich frag mich wie. Daß die Schwal-
> ben über dem Bohnenfeld, aufgefädelt in den Wolken, die gleichen
> Flügelspitzen wie Nelus Schnurrbart haben, ist unbegreiflich, aber nur
> ein Fehler. Wie bei allen Fehlern krieg ich nicht heraus, ob die Gegen-
> stände oder die Gedanken es so haben wollen. Da es so ist, müßte der
> Verstand den Fehlern gewachsen sein, so viele tragen können wie die
> Erde Bäume. (*HB*, 111 f.)

To simply reject an unpalatable reality may seem like an admission of defeat, and Herta Müller's micro-politics of resistance may often appear not to be a politics at all, so much as an *anti*-politics. When Irene is asked by the West German official whether she had wanted to bring down the government in 'das andere Land', for example, she astonishes the reader by answering in the negative, though everything about her bespeaks her dissidence (*RB*, 28). She and her interlocutor speak past each other, he assuming that a political person must have goals and presumably be part of a

group, she asserting the baseline value of gut opposition in the
face of monumental power. Müller's unceasing defence of the individual against systems which crush them is undoubtedly in the
tradition of the emancipatory discourses of the Enlightenment, but
her privileging of the detail and of the contingent over grand
narratives and hierarchies, her defence of desire and refusal to
privilege 'Verstand'[26] are also profoundly modern, not to say postmodern, and are equally, though differently, political. I mean this
in the sense in which Thomas Docherty, drawing on Levinas, re-
defines the political in the age of postmodernism:

> We can no longer legislate comfortably between opposing or compet-
> ing political systems, for we no longer subscribe to any such totalising
> forms; but we can address the instance, the events, of justice. [. . .]
> We must behave justly towards the face of the Other; but we cannot
> do that according to a predetermined system of justice, a predetermin-
> ed political theory. [. . .] The demand is for a just relating to alterity,
> and for a cognition of the event of heterogeneity. In short, therefore,
> we must discover – produce – justice. It is here that the real political
> burden and trajectory of the postmodern is to be found: the search for
> a just politics, or the search for just a politics.[27]

Some reviewers of her work in Germany have of late tended to
accuse Müller of artistic stagnation[28] and have urged her to high-
light the many injustices perpetrated under Western democracies-
rather than continuing to flog the dead horse of totalitarianism.[29]
But the recent international recognition accorded to *The Land of
Green Plums*, the English translation of *Herztier*, in the award of
the Dublin-IMPAC prize is testament to the fact that, despite the
dramatic fall of the Eastern European regimes which are Müller's
particular *bêtes noires*, as long as there exists a single country
which can be described as 'a prison without bars', as a recent
Amnesty International report described Burma[30] (and there are
currently many), writing which investigates and celebrates resistance through the God of Small Things will demand our urgent
attention.

Notes

[1] Ruth Klüger, *weiter leben* (Göttingen, Wallstein, 1992).
[2] 'Meine Jahre mit Helmut Kohl', *Die Zeit*, 2 September 1994, 56;

'Sarkuhi ist unschuldig. Wie halten wir es mit der Freiheit des Geistes? Ein Appell', *Die Zeit*, 1 August 1997.

[3] See for example Ulrich Schreiber, 'Von der Schuld der Sprache in einer gewalttätigen Welt. Podiumsdiskussion mit Grass, Müller u.a. auf der Tagung des westdeutschen PEN-Zentrums', *Frankfurter Rundschau*, 21 May 1994; anon, 'Neue Proteste gegen Friedenspreis des deutschen Buchhandels für Annemarie Schimmel. Autoren raten dem Bundespräsidenten Herzog von der Verleihung ab. Kritik an Orientalistin bekräftigt', *Stuttgarter Zeitung*, 6 September 1995, 25; anon, 'Massimo-Stipendiaten. Anderson soll wegbleiben', *Frankfurter Rundschau*, 25 December 1991, 11. Other newspaper articles on these topics are listed in the bibliography.

[4] Sibylle Cramer, for example, condemns what she sees as 'die Taufe der Gelegenheitsarbeiten zu Essays' in *Hunger und Seide* as 'ein Schwindel': Sibylle Cramer, 'Richtige Worte, falsche Taufen. Traktate einer Moralistin. Herta Müllers publizistische Gelegenheitsarbeiten, als Essays präsentiert', *Süddeutsche Zeitung*, 10/11 June 1995; Hannelore Schlaffer accuses Müller of an 'unerbittliche[] moralische[] Integrität' which is inappropriate to the post-communist world: 'Ihre zornige Empire stammt aus einer Epoche, die immer ferner rückt': Hannelore Schlaffer, 'Liegt Deutschland in Rumänien? Herta Müllers gesammelte Berichte und Reden über das beschädigte Leben in den Diktaturen: *Hunger und Seide*', *Frankfurter Rundschau*, 21 March 1995, 25.

[5] Martin Krumbholz, 'Vom Umgang mit der Angst', *Süddeutsche Zeitung*, 30 January 1997.

[6] For Müller's moving tribute to her friend, see 'Das kleingewürfelte Glück. Erinnerung an den Dichter Rolf Bossert', *Frankfurter Allgemeine Zeitung*, 17 February 1996, 27.

[7] Friedmar Apel has noted similarities between Müller's instinctual resistance and the Romantics' prizing of 'Eigensinn': Friedmar Apel, 'Schreiben, Trennen. Zur Poetik des eigensinnigen Blicks bei Herta Müller', in Norbert Otto Eke (ed.), *Die erfundene Wahrnehmung*, 22–7, here 22 f. See also his description elsewhere of the narrator of *Herztier*: 'im anderen Blick übt sie die Widerständigkeit und den Eigensinn eines gegen alle Einsicht autonom sein wollenden Individuums und weiß doch, daß die aus dieser Perspektive wahrgenommene fremde Verlorenheit im Grunde auch die eigene ist': 'Turbatverse. Ästhetik, Mystik und Politik bei Herta Müller', *Akzente*, 44 No. 2 (1997), 113–25, here 123.

[8] Norbert Otto Eke, '"Sein Leben machen / ist nicht, / sein Glück machen / mein Herr". Zum Verhältnis von Ästhetik und Politik in Herta Müllers Nachrichten aus Rumänien', *Jahrbuch der Deutschen Schillergesellschaft*, 41 (1997), 481–509, here 509.

[9] Elias Canetti, *Masse und Macht* (1960) (Frankfurt am Main, Fischer, 1980), 249.

[10] Quoted in Denis Staunton, 'The spy who loved me', *The Guardian*, 7 July 1998; this recollection incidentally found its way into *Der Fuchs war damals schon der Jäger*, where Paul has a similar reaction to the death of the *Conducator* and his wife: 'ich ekle mich vor ihnen, und ich muß um sie weinen. Woher kommt dieses Mitleid' (*FJ*, 277).

[11] See this volume, 22 f.

[12] Ibid., 17.

[13] Ibid., 21.

[14] This does not make the task of the reader easy, for, to quote Naomi Schor paraphrasing Sir Joshua Reynolds in his defence of the Sublime, 'By dividing and dispersing the spectator's attention [. . .] the detail blocks the dynamic rush of the Imagination, fatigues the eye, and in the end induces anxiety rather than the elevating pleasure of the Sublime': Naomi Schor, *Reading in Detail: Aesthetics and the Feminine* (New York; London, Methuen, 1987), 19. Müller of course works productively with the blocking, anxiety-producing function of the detail. As such her work contributes to the 'ongoing valorization of the detail' which is 'an essential aspect of that dismantling of Idealist metaphysics which looms so large on the agenda of modernity', Shor, *Reading in Detail*, 3 f.

[15] See this volume, 15 f.

[16] See David Midgley's and Ricarda Schmidt's contributions to this volume for further elaboration of this process.

[17] 'Dennoch kann es vorkommen, daß Müller in ihrem Ziel, Uniformität zu denunzieren, selbst in die Geste homogenisierender Metaphorik verfällt [. . .]: Der SS-Vater machte Friedhöfe, sonst nichts': this volume, 72.

[18] Eke, '"Sein Leben machen"', 509.

[19] Stephan Düppe, 'Geschicke der Schrift als Strategien subjektiver Ohnmacht. Zu Herta Müllers poetologischen Vorlesungen *Der Teufel sitzt im Spiegel*, in Ralph Köhnen (ed.), *Der Druck der Erfahrung treibt die Sprache in die Dichtung. Bildlichkeit in Texten Herta Müllers* (Frankfurt am Main, Lang, 1997), 155–69, here 167.

[20] See this volume, 22.

[21] See this volume, 71.

[22] The factory work and the regular interrogations are taken from Müller's direct experience, as is the incident with the hair (see below), though this 'Ich' is not an intellectual.

[23] For an elaboration of the layers of political history behind Müller's texts see John J. White's contribution to this volume, here 76.

[24] Müller has no time for feminism, pointing out that women are everywhere complicit in abuses of power (for example she opened her speech at a conference on 'Der Sozialismus und die Frau' with the words 'Elena Ceauşescu war eine Frau': Swansea Department video, 6 October 1996). However she has catalogued the appalling ways in which the Ceauşescu regime controlled and endangered women's lives through the regulation of reproduction (*HS*, 78–85), and painted sympathetic portraits of the sexual exploitation of women in the figures of Amalie in *Der Mensch ist ein großer Fasan auf der Welt* and Lola in *Herztier*.

[25] Elsewhere Müller has written about meeting her own interrogator again after the fall of the regime (who in this version of the incident did replace the hair and then let her go); though he was now insecure and fearful and she was no longer afraid of him, the past could not be undone: she could think of nothing to say to put him in his place, and he was still the same man: 'Die frische Ohnmacht in seinem Gesicht ist

nichts als die verglühte Macht von damals': 'Das Haar auf der Schulter. Fünf Texte zur Messe in C-Dur von Franz Schubert', *Frankfurter Rundschau*, 26/27 May 1996.

[26] One of the most life-affirming passages in *Reisende auf einem Bein* is when Thomas explicitly rejects the domination of 'Verstand': 'Manchmal könnte man meinen, wir haben keinen Verstand. Und brauchen auch keinen. Nur sinnliche Kraft, um zu leben. Weißt du, wo man das merkt, auf windigen Straßen, auf Bahnsteigen im Freien und auf Brücken. Dort bewegen die Menschen sich so schamlos und leicht, daß sie den Himmel fast berühren' (*RB*, 132 f.).

[27] Thomas Docherty, 'Postmodernism: an introduction', in Thomas Docherty (ed.), *Postmodernism: A Reader* (New York; London, Harvester Wheatsheaf, 1993), 1–31, here 26 f.

[28] See for example Hannes Krauss, 'Innenansichten', *Freitag*, 10 October 1997; also Ernst Osterkamp, 'Das verkehrte Glück. Herta Müllers Roman aus der Diktatur', *Frankfurter Allgemeine Zeitung*, 14 October 1997.

[29] Sabine Kebir, 'So rot wie ein Beet Klatschmohn. Immer wieder Rumänien. Herta Müllers fortgesetzte Rückschau auf die Zeit der Diktatur', *die tageszeitung*, 15 October 1997, 9.

[30] Amnesty International, *Myanmar: Conditions in Prisons and Labour Camps*, AI Index, ASA 16/22/95, 22 September 1995, quoted in John Pilger, *Hidden Agendas* (London, Vintage, 1998), 158.

10

Bibliography 1990–1998

OWEN EVANS

This bibliography is a continuation of Dagmar Eke's in Norbert Otto Eke (ed.), *Die erfundene Wahrnehmung. Annäherung an Herta Müller* (Paderborn, Igel, 1991), 134–57, which covers the period 1972–90. Entries have been arranged by year and subdivided into the following sections: primary; secondary – general literary studies and specific book reviews; secondary – miscellaneous; interviews. The primary references are ordered as follows: books; books in translation; articles in books and journals; articles and prose in newspapers and radio broadcasts arranged chronologically. All other entries are arranged alphabetically according to the author's surname. Page numbers of newspaper articles have been given where possible. The compiler's comments are in square brackets. The compiler would like to acknowledge the assistance of the *Deutsches Literaturarchiv*, Marbach, and the Innsbruck *Zeitungsarchiv* in producing this bibliography.

1990

1. Primary

Barfüßiger Februar. Prosa (Berlin, Rotbuch, 1990) [first published Berlin, Rotbuch, 1987].

'Heimat oder der Betrug der Dinge', in Wilhelm Solms (ed.), *Dichtung und Heimat. Sieben Autoren unterlaufen ein Thema* (Marburg, Hitzeroth, 1990), 69–83.

'Zwischen den Häusern ist nichts. Paralipomena aus *Niederungen*', in Wilhelm Solms (ed.), *Nachruf auf die rumäniendeutsche Literatur* (Marburg, Hitzeroth, 1990), 67–76 [extract from *Niederungen*].

'Der Regen', *Hermannstädter Zeitung*, 12 January 1990, 5.

'Bayern, deine Sterne. Ein Zwischenruf', *Die Zeit*, 25 May 1990.

'Hunger und Seide. Die Hilflosigkeit der Sklavensprache. Weshalb Ceauşescus Schrecken seinen Tod überlebt hat', *Frankfurter Allgemeine Zeitung*, 16 June 1990 [revised and extended version entitled 'Hunger und Seide. Männer und Frauen im Alltag' reprinted in *Hunger und Seide. Essays* (Reinbek bei Hamburg, Rowohlt, 1994), 65–87].

'Auf den Trümmern der Revolution', *Zeitmagazin*, 6 July 1990, 8–14 [revised and extended version entitled 'Soldaten schossen in die Luft – die Luft nur war in den Lungen. Temeswar nach der Revolution' reprinted in *Hunger und Seide*, 115–26].

'Lügen haben kurze Beine – die Wahrheit hat keine. Das wahre Engagement in der Fälschung', *Die Zeit*, 20 July 1990 [reprinted in *Hunger und Seide*, 107–14].

'Zopf aus Fleisch', *Deutsche Volkszeitung*, 20 July 1990, 13.

'Barfüßiger Februar', *Hermannstädter Zeitung*, 26 October 1990, 5 [prose extract].

'Geschichten einer nicht Erwünschten', *Neues Deutschland*, 15/16 December 1990, 14 [includes the following texts: (i) 'Was ich mal fragen wollte', (ii) 'Verdächtigrot', (iii) 'Die Rumkugel', (iv) 'Der wilde Hang', (v) 'Die Münzen', (vi) 'Von der Wachsamkeit gebissen zu werden'].

2. Secondary: General Literary Studies and Specific Book Reviews

Anon, '*Reisende auf einem Bein*', *Volksstimmung*, 27 February 1990.

Dietze, Gabriele, 'Über Herta Müller', *Börsenblatt*, 7 December 1990, 3895–7.

Marin, Marcel, '"Ja, Angst". Ein Porträt der in West-Berlin lebenden Schriftstellerin Herta Müller nach der Revolution in ihrem Heimatstaat Rumänien', *Eßlinger Zeitung*, 27/28 January 1990, 33.

Stöberer, Heinrich, 'Nicht mehr dort und noch nicht da', *Kronen-Zeitung*, 28 February 1990 [on *Reisende*].

Stromberg, Kyra, '*Reisende auf einem Bein*', Deutsche Welle, 11 January 1990 [review on the 'Lesezeichen' programme].

3. Secondary: Miscellaneous

Anon, 'Sorge um Rumänien. Herta Müller in der Alten Feuerwache', *Kölner Stadt-Anzeiger*, 14 February 1990.

Anon, 'In fremder Heimat. Schriftstellerin Herta Müller las in Mannheim', *Mannheimer Morgen*, 17/18 March 1990, 36.

Anon, 'Auszeichnung für Herta Müller', *Salzburger Nachrichten*, 28 June 1990 [Herta Müller wins the *Roswitha-Medaille der Stadt Gandersheim*].

Anon, 'Eine Schilderung verlorener Welten. Herta Müller, Freya Klier und Irene Dische sprechen über ihre Deutschlandbilder', *Süddeutsche Zeitung*, 26 November 1990, 32 [preview of ZDF documentary film 'Verlorene Welten. Blicke auf Deutschland heute', directed by Jutta Szostak, featuring Herta Müller].

Braunschweig-Ullmann, Renate, 'Dialog der fremden Freunde. Das zweite europäische Literaturtreffen in Straßburg', *Schwäbische Zeitung*, 15 November 1990 [Herta Müller is one of those taking part].

Emmerling, Eugen, '"Warum die Angst, wenn irgendwo etwas Fremdes auftaucht?". Literarischer Abend des Börsenvereins in Bonn mit der rumäniendeutschen Autorin Herta Müller', *Börsenblatt*, 7 December 1990, 3894–5.

Frederiksen, Anne, 'Fremd das Land', *Die Zeit*, 23 November 1990, 76 [preview of 'Verlorene Welten'].

Pieper, Heidrun, 'Die Fremdheit blieb. Herta Müller las im Haus des Deutschen Ostens', *Rheinische Post*, 22 September 1990.

Richard, Christine, 'Achtung, es herrscht Sturzgefahr! Die rumäniendeutsche Autorin Herta Müller in Basel', *Basler Zeitung*, 12 April 1990.

Rüb, Matthias, 'Leben an einem gefährlichen Ort. Drei Autorinnen werfen "Blicke auf Deutschland"', *Frankfurter Allgemeine Zeitung*, 28 November 1990, 34 [preview of 'Verlorene Welten'].

Urban-Halle, Peter, 'Der fremde Freund. Ein deutsches Schriftstellertreffen in Straßburg', *Der Tagesspiegel*, 15 November 1990, 4.

Vogt, Heribert, 'Die Dinge und die Namen. Herta Müller las in der Mannheimer Kunsthalle', *Rhein-Neckar-Zeitung*, 21 March 1990, 9.

4. Interviews

Jakobs, Karl-Heinz, 'Das Wort "Heimat" beanspruche ich nicht für mich', *Neues Deutschland*, 15/16 December 1990, 14.
Uhrte, Ferenc and Béla Szende, 'Blick über die Maisfelder hinaus. Gespräch mit Herta Müller und Richard Wagner', *Neue Zeitung*, 24 March 1990, 8–9.
Urbach, Karina, 'Gästebett in Deutschland. Die Fremdheit ist geblieben', *Münchner Merkur*, 28 March 1990.

1991

1. Primary

Der Teufel sitzt im Spiegel. Wie Wahrnehmung sich erfindet (Berlin, Rotbuch, 1991).
En tierras bajas, translated by Juan José del Solar (Madrid, Siruela, 1991) [Spanish translation of *Niederungen*].
'Die Stirnlocke. Auszug aus dem Roman mit dem Arbeitstitel "Füchse gehen in die Falle"', *Neue Deutsche Literatur*, 39 No. 12 (1991), 9–25.
'Der Staub ist blind – die Sonne ein Krüppel. Beleidigt, verfolgt und ins Elend gestoßen. Zur Lage der Zigeuner in Rumänien', *Frankfurter Allgemeine Zeitung*, 4 May 1991 [reprinted in *Hunger und Seide*, 136–53].
'Wie Wahrnehmung sich erfindet. Poetische Überlegungen zum Prozeß des Schreibens', *Frankfurter Rundschau*, 11 May 1991.
'Eine Lüge, vor der man friert. Nach dem versuchten Staatsstreich in der Sowjetunion: Eine Umfrage unter ausländischen und deutschen Schriftstellern', *Frankfurter Allgemeine Zeitung*, 21 August 1991 [contribution from Herta Müller].
'Schreiben', *Neues Deutschland*, 6 December 1991, 10 [extract from *Der Teufel*].
'Das Land am Nebentisch', *Neue Zürcher Zeitung*, 6 December 1991, 41–2; also in *Hermannstädter Zeitung*, 8 May 1992, 5.
'Ahnungen sehen Tatsachen blind', *Frankfurter Allgemeine Zeitung*, 7 December 1991; also in *Karpaten-Rundschau*, 23 January 1992, 4–5.

'Sie zittern vor Kälte und beten nicht. Zwei Jahre danach: Am Grabe Ceauşescus', *Frankfurter Allgemeine Zeitung*, 28 December 1991, 25.

2. Secondary: General Literary Studies and Specific Book Reviews

Anon, '*Der Teufel sitzt im Spiegel*', *Der kleine Bund*, 19 October 1991, 4.

Appelt, Hedwig, 'Sinnenpanorama. Herta Müllers Poetik', *Stuttgarter Zeitung*, 20 December 1991, 22 [on *Der Teufel*].

Auffermann, Verena, 'Der Zeigefinger im Kopf. Herta Müllers Poetik-Vorlesungen', *Süddeutsche Zeitung*, 13/14 July 1991 [on *Der Teufel*].

David, Horst, 'Herta Müller und die Rumäniendeutschen', *Karpaten-Rundschau*, 31 October 1991, 4–5.

Eke, Norbert Otto (ed.), *Die erfundene Wahrnehmung. Annäherung an Herta Müller* (Paderborn, Igel, 1991).

Eke, Norbert Otto, '*Reisende auf einem Bein* und *Der Teufel sitzt im Spiegel. Wie Wahrnehmung sich erfindet*', *Halbasien*, 1 No. 2 (1991), 67–72.

Huther, Christian, 'Schreiben als Gegenteil von Leben. Herta Müllers Reflexionen zu Literatur und Politik', *Der Tagesspiegel*, 22 September 1991, 9 [on *Der Teufel*].

Huther, Christian, '*Der Teufel sitzt im Spiegel*. Herta Müllers Reflexionen zu Literatur und Politik', *General-Anzeiger*, 26/27 October 1991, 11 [revised version of *Tagesspiegel* review].

Janssen-Zimmermann, Antje, '"Überall, wo man den Tod gesehen hat, ist man ein bißchen wie zuhaus". Schreiben nach Auschwitz. Zu einer Erzählung Herta Müllers', *Literatur für Leser* (1991), No. 4, 237–49 [on *Barfüßiger Februar*].

Kretzen, Friederike, 'Poetik der Fremdheit. *Der Teufel sitzt im Spiegel*. Herta Müllers masslose Sätze', *Basler Zeitung*, 30 August 1991, 46.

Matt, Beatrice von, 'Die innere und die äußere Wahrnehmung. Ein Lektürehinweis zum Text von Herta Müller', *Neue Zürcher Zeitung*, 6 December 1991, 41 [accompanies 'Das Land am Nebentisch'].

Mayer, Susanne, 'Ein Erdhauch über Gräbern. Herta Müllers Poetik-Vorlesungen *Der Teufel sitzt im Spiegel*', *Die Zeit*, 11 October 1991, 10–11.

Meidinger-Geise, Inge, 'Der Teufel sitzt im Spiegel', *Südostdeutsche Vierteljahresblätter*, 40 No. 4 (1991), 334–5.

Mings, Ute, 'Der Teufel sitzt im Spiegel', Sender Freies Berlin, 18 December 1991 [radio review on the 'Buchzeit' programme].

Sastre, Roberto Fernández, 'Nueva savia expresionista. *En tierras bajas*. Herta Müller', *El Pais*, 12 March 1991, 2 [review of *Niederungen*].

Schirrmacher, Frank, 'In jedem Haus nur einen Augenblick bleiben. Herta Müllers Essays über die Entstehung der Literatur aus Angst', *Frankfurter Allgemeine Zeitung*, 3 August 1991 [on *Der Teufel*].

Schnetz, Wolf Peter, 'Denkprosa von Herta Müller', *Der Literat*, 33 No. 10 (1991), 26–7 [on *Der Teufel*].

3. Secondary: Miscellaneous

Anon, 'Diktatur in Rumänien. Warnung rumäniendeutscher Autoren', *Frankfurter Allgemeine Zeitung*, 16 February 1991, 25 [including comments by Herta Müller].

Anon, 'Die fortwährende Flucht. Herta Müller las unveröffentlichte poetische Prosa', *Schwäbisches Tagblatt*, 10 May 1991 [on 'Das Land am Nebentisch'].

Anon, 'Beste Bücher und ein Ärgernis – im August. Empfehlung und Verfehlung – was von den Kritikern der *Frankfurter Allgemeine Zeitung* im vergangenen Monat besonders hervorgehoben wurde', *Frankfurter Allgemeine Zeitung*, 4 September 1991 [brief reference to *Der Teufel*].

Anon, 'Kranich mit dem Stein. Literaturpreis an Herta Müller', *Frankfurter Allgemeine Zeitung*, 30 September 1991, 33 [Herta Müller awarded the Kranichsteiner Prize].

Anon, 'Massimo-Stipendiaten. Anderson soll wegbleiben', *Frankfurter Rundschau*, 25 December 1991, 11 [Herta Müller amongst others signs a statement opposing Sascha Anderson's scholarship to the German Cultural Centre in Rome].

Baron, Ulrich, 'Literatur im Zeichen des Kranichs. In der Berliner Akademie der Künste wurden Herta Müller, Ginka Steinwachs und die Übersetzerin Eva Mildenhauer ausgezeichnet', *Rheinischer Merkur*, 4 October 1991, 23.

Gutschke, Irmtraud, 'Kein Literaturzirkus, ein subtiles Gespräch über Texte. Der traditionsreiche Wettbewerb um den "Kranich mit dem Stein" zum ersten Mal in Berlin', *Neues Deutschland*, 1 October 1991.

Liebscher, Thomas, '"Literatur lebt zum Großteil von Erinnerung". Mit ihrer Übersiedlung vom Banat nach Berlin hat Herta Müller ihr Thema nicht verloren', *Badische Neueste Nachrichten*, 13 May 1991, 13.

Mack, Gerhard, 'Literatur braucht Geduld. Vierzehn Autoren haben während der "Erzählzeit in Singen" ihre Texte vorgestellt', *Stuttgarter Zeitung*, 15 May 1991, 29 [Herta Müller is one of those participating].

Ramm, Klaus J., 'Identität, Entwurzelung und Schreiben. Deutsch-indisches Autorentreffen in LCB und Haus der Kulturen', *Der Tagesspiegel*, 14 September 1991, 16 [Herta Müller read 'Das Land am Nebentisch' and the *Schlußrede*].

Ross, Jan, 'Schwierigkeit beim Lesen. Unbeholfene Juroren. Kranichsteiner Literaturtage in Berlin', *Frankfurter Allgemeine Zeitung*, 1 October 1991, 33.

Samain, Thea, 'Vage Welt aus klaren Tränen. Herta Müller gewann den Kranich mit dem Stein', *Neue Zeit*, 5 October 1991, 14.

Staudacher, Cornelia, 'Das Schwarze im Auge des Diktators. Erstmals in Berlin veranstaltet: die Kranichsteiner Literaturtage. Herta Müller für *Die Stirnlocke* ausgezeichnet', *Der Tagesspiegel*, 1 October 1991.

Staudacher, Cornelia, 'Angst macht Menschen wieder zu Kindern', *Saarbrücker Zeitung*, 19 November 1991, 19.

Tschapke, Reinhard, 'Poetische Initiative von unten. Eine VS-Konkurrenz?', *Die Welt*, 2 October 1991, 27 [on the meeting of a new writers' group including Herta Müller].

Wichner, Ernest, 'Kranichsteiner Literaturtage in Berlin. Die Jury entschied richtig', *Basler Zeitung*, 2 October 1991.

4. Interviews

Soldt, Rüdiger, 'Fremder als eine Deutsche in Rumänien. Ein Gespräch mit der Schriftstellerin Herta Müller über Konsum- und Mangelgesellschaften, über ihr Heimatland und Osteuropa', *Badische Zeitung*, 20/21 April 1991, 5.

Soldt, Rüdiger, 'Nur ein Überleben. Ein Interview mit Herta Müller über antastbare Würde in Überfluß und Mangel, die rumänische Revolution und ihre Auflösung', *Die Tageszeitung*, 27 April 1991.

1992

1. Primary

Der Fuchs war damals schon der Jäger. *Roman* (Reinbek bei Hamburg, Rowohlt, 1992).

Reisende auf einem Bein (Berlin, Rotbuch, 1992) [first published Berlin, Rotbuch, 1989].

Eine warme Kartoffel ist ein warmes Bett. Kolumnen 1990–92 (Hamburg, Europäische Verlagsanstalt, 1992).

In viaggio su una gamba sola, translated by Lidia Castellani (Venice, Marsilio, 1992) [Italian translation of *Reisende auf einem Bein*].

The Passport, translated by Martin Chalmers (London, Serpent's Tail, 1992) [English translation of *Der Mensch ist ein großer Fasan auf der Welt*, first published in English London, Serpent's Tail, 1989].

'Der Einbruch eines staatlichen Auftrags in die Familie. Frauentag und Diktatur', Hessischer Rundfunk, 8 May 1992 [radio essay published in *Hunger und Seide*, 101–4].

'Autoren lesen ihre Lieblingsautoren. 4. Teil. Herta Müller liest Rolf Bossert', Bayerischer Rundfunk, 26 June 1992 [on the 'Die Geschichte der Woche' programme].

'Wenn der Vollmond dies alles bescheinigt. Was die Direktorin der Villa Massimo unter Kunstforderung versteht und warum die Künstler darunter leiden', *Frankfurter Allgemeine Zeitung*, 29 June 1992, 30.

'Das friedliche Zuschauen beim Krieg', Südwestfunk, 6 September 1992 [radio essay on the 'Blick in die Zeit' programme].

'Die Tage werden weitergehen. Nur eine militärische Intervention könnte die serbische Aggression stoppen', *die tageszeitung*, 8 September 1992, 14 [reprinted in *Hunger und Seide*, 157–63].

'Schmeckt das Rattengift? Von der Hinterhältigkeit der Güte zur Beweglichkeit des Hasses. Eine Momentaufnahme aus dem wiedervereinigten Deutschland', *Frankfurter Rundschau*, 31 October 1992 [reprinted in *Hunger und Seide*, 39–49].

2. Secondary: General Literary Studies and Specific Book Reviews

Anon, 'Schrecken der Bilder', *Der Spiegel*, 24 August 1992 , 216 [on *Der Fuchs*].

Appelt, Hedwig, 'Viele rührige Wesen. Reichlich bemühte Bilder', *Stuttgarter Zeitung*, 11 September 1992, 24 [on *Der Fuchs*].

Assheuer, Thomas, '"Auf der Stirn des Diktators sitzt eine Blattlaus und stellt sich tot". Der rumänische Sozialismus als Höhlengleichnis. Herta Müllers Abrechnung *Der Fuchs war damals schon der Jäger*', *Frankfurter Rundschau*, 15 August 1992.

Auffermann, Verena, 'Schatten der Securitate. Porträt einer Chronistin der Diktatur', *Profil*, 28 September 1992, 4–6.

Auffermann, Verena, 'Wo bei anderen das Herz ist, ist bei denen ein Friedhof. Herta Müllers Roman über die Angst, die Staatssicherheit und das Ende das Diktators Ceauşescu', *Süddeutsche Zeitung*, 30 September 1992 [on *Der Fuchs*].

Cosack, Bettina, 'Es läßt sich schwer erzählen von den Würfeln im Schädel. Herta Müllers neuer Roman *Der Fuchs war damals schon der Jäger*', *Berliner Zeitung*, 9 October 1992, 31.

Dattenberger, Simone, 'Filz aus Elend und Staatsterror. Herta Müllers neuer Roman *Der Fuchs war damals schon der Jäger*', *Münchner Merkur*, 12 November 1992.

Eggebrecht, Harald, 'Alle fürchten den Absturz. Herta Müllers mitleidlose Beschreibung der Diktatur', *Wochenpost*, 1 October 1992, 20 [on *Der Fuchs*].

Filip, Ota, 'Geblendete, Gedemütigte, Gebrandmarkte – Liebe und Verrat zweier Freundinnen in Ceauşescus Rumänien', *Die Welt am Sonntag*, 27 September 1992, 2 [on *Der Fuchs*].

Fitzel, Thomas, 'Überwintern in der Diktatur. Herta Müllers Roman über Wahrnehmung von Armseligkeit, Monotonie und Fremdheit', *Neue Zeit*, 4 November 1992, 14 [on *Der Fuchs* and *Der Teufel*].

Gargano, Antonella, 'Herta Müllers Poetik', *Studi Germanici*, (1992/93), No. 30/31, 399–408.

Gohlis, Tobias, 'Der Hauch der Angst', *Hannoversche Allgemeine Zeitung*, 29 September 1992 [on *Der Fuchs*].

Gohlis, Tobias, 'Das Schwarze im Auge des Diktators. Innenansichten eines totalitären Regimes. Die Rumäniendeutsche Herta Müller beschreibt in ihrem neuen Roman das Leben im Ceauşescu-Staat', *Rheinischer Merkur*, 4 December 1992, 34; also in *Karpaten-Rundschau*, 8 February 1993, 4–5 [on *Der Fuchs* and *Warme Kartoffel*].

Heyl, Thomas, 'Kleine Welten, großes Grauen. Herta Müllers neuer Roman hält die letzten Wochen der Diktatur Ceauşescus fest', *Falter*, 2 October 1992, 15 [on *Der Fuchs*].

Hintermeier, Hannes, 'Überleben war eben alles', *Konturen* (1992), No. 3, 75–6 [on *Der Fuchs*].

Hoffmann, Christian, 'Wolken der Langeweile. Herta Müllers neuer Roman verwirrt seine Leser', *Wiener Zeitung*, 11 September 1992 [on *Der Fuchs*].

Jäger, Manfred, 'Nervenkrieg in finsterer Zeit. In ihrem Roman *Der Fuchs war damals schon der Jäger* erzählt Herta Müller vom Leben mit der Diktatur. Das Rumänien Ceauşescus – ein Kosmos der alltäglichen Grausamkeiten, wo selbst ein Haustier zum Verwirrspiel der Spitzel gehört', *Deutsches Allgemeines Sonntagsblatt*, 30 October 1992, 28.

Keim, Stefan, '*Der Fuchs war damals schon der Jäger*', Westdeutscher Rundfunk, 22 October 1992 [review on the 'Meinungen über Bücher' programme].

Krauss, Hannes, 'Jäger-Schnipsel. Herta Müllers Roman *Der Fuchs war damals schon der Jäger*', *Freitag*, 2 October 1992, 27.

Kretzen, Friederike, 'Schutz ist Täuschung. Adina lebt hier nicht mehr. Herta Müllers *Der Fuchs war damals schon der Jäger*', *Tages Anzeiger*, 30 September 1992.

Küchler, Sabine and Christine Richard, 'Nachrichten aus einem Land, in dem sogar die Pappeln Messer waren. Briefwechsel über Bücher III. Über *Der Fuchs war damals schon der Jäger* von Herta Müller', *Basler Zeitung*, 30 September 1992, 9.

Laudenbach, Peter, 'Unter die Haut gewachsen. Kein Aufatmen nach Ceauşescu. Herta Müllers Roman *Der Fuchs war damals schon der Jäger*', *Die Tageszeitung*, 30 September 1992.

Lodron, Herbert, 'Die Pappeln sind Messer. Düster-Surrealistisches von Herta Müller', *Die Presse*, 14 August 1992 [on *Der Fuchs*].

Matt, Peter von, 'Diktatur und Dichtung. Herta Müllers Gedanken über Fuchs und Jäger', *Frankfurter Allgemeine Zeitung*, 29 September 1992 [on *Der Fuchs*].

Mitgutsch, Waltraud Anna, 'Die Verfolgung kann weitergehen', *Der Standard*, 11 September 1992 [on *Der Fuchs*].

Morlang, Werner, 'Das Prinzip Unruhe. Zu Herta Müllers Buch *Der Teufel sitzt im Spiegel*', *Tages Anzeiger*, 19 March 1992.

Motzan, Peter, 'Fuchsjagd durch die Straßen der Nacht. Herta Müllers Roman über Rumänien', *Die Welt*, 28 November 1992, 25; also in *Karpaten-Rundschau*, 1 January 1993, 4–5 [on *Der Fuchs*].

Panic, Ira, 'Kampflüstige Dissidentin. Die deutsch-rumänische Schriftstellerin Herta Müller beschreibt in ihrem neuen Roman *Der Fuchs war damals schon der Jäger* Folter, Verrat und Todesangst im Ceauşescu-Staat', *Stern*, 15 October 1992, 320–2.

Parschalk, Volkmar, '*Der Fuchs war damals schon der Jäger*', Österreichischer Rundfunk, 27 December 1992 [review on the 'Ex Libris' programme].

Raddatz, Fritz J., 'Pinzetten-Prosa. Film-Szenen statt Erzähl-Garten. Woran Herta Müllers Roman scheiterte', *Die Zeit*, 28 August 1992, 57; also in *Karpaten-Rundschau*, 10 September 1992, 4–5 [on *Der Fuchs*].

Schweizer-Meyer, Barbara, 'Das Fragmentieren der Wirklichkeit. Herta Müller: *Der Fuchs war damals schon der Jäger*', *Neue Zürcher Zeitung*, 21 August 1992, 29.

Staudacher, Cornelia, 'Die Verrohung des Menschen unter einem totalitären Regime. Herta Müllers poetische Paraphrase über das Leben in der Diktatur: *Der Fuchs war damals schon der Jäger*', *Der Tagesspiegel*, 29 September 1992.

Staudacher, Cornelia, 'Schwäbin, Rumänin, Deutsche. Wer nachdenkt, ist nirgends zu Hause. Die Schriftstellerin Herta Müller', *Der Tagesspiegel*, 13 December 1992, 22.

Trumpf, Torsten, 'Herta Müller. Autorin aus dem Banat', *Prager Zeitung*, 26 May 1992.

3. Secondary: Miscellaneous

Anon, 'Tote Villa', *Rheinischer Merkur*, 3 July 1992 [response to Herta Müller's article of 29 June 1992 in the *Frankfurter Allgemeine Zeitung*].

Angermann, Constanze, 'Fremde Sprache, vertrauter Rhythmus. Herta Müller und Nicole Bary berichten über die Arbeit des Übersetzens', *Frankfurter Rundschau*, 14 February 1992, 20.

Böttiger, Helmut, 'Achtung, Pinzette! Zu einer Lesung Herta Müllers', *Frankfurter Rundschau*, 9 November 1992, 12.

Buselmeier, Michael, 'Stasi, bleiche Mutter. Zeitschriftenrundschau', *Frankfurter Rundschau*, 21 March 1992 [survey of reactions to intellectuals who were 'Spitzel', and refers to Herta Müller's attitude to Sascha Anderson].

Geißler, Cornelia, 'Natürlich wird das den Haß nicht besänftigen. Herta Müller sprach im "Studio LCB" von ihrer Angst in dieser Zeit', *Berliner Zeitung*, 9 November 1992, 31.

Hieber, Jochen, '*Der Fuchs war damals schon der Jäger*. Herta Müllers Roman als Vorabdruck in der *F.A.Z*', *Frankfurter Allgemeine Zeitung*, 7 July 1992, 27.

Hintermeier, Hannes, 'Wer Feuer legt, will töten. Gespräche mit Umberto Eco, Libuše Moníková, Herta Müller und Coraghessan Boyle', *Arbeiter Zeitung*, 2/3/4 October 1992, 9.

Iuga, Nora, 'Ich bin nirgends zu Hause. Herta Müller im Kreuzfeuer der Fragen', *Karpaten-Rundschau*, 23 January 1992, 4.

Linder, Gisela, 'Frei vom Wildwuchs des Privaten. Vier Autorinnen bei den Literaturtagen in Meersburg', *Schwäbische Zeitung*, 25 May 1992 [including Herta Müller].

Lohr, Horst, '*Der Fuchs war damals schon der Jäger*. Im Theaterhaus. Die Schriftstellerin Herta Müller liest aus einem noch unveröffentlichten Text', *Stuttgarter Nachrichten*, 17 February 1992, 11.

Polaczek, Dieter, 'Die Leiden der jungen Künstler. Posse und Polemik. Der Streit um die Villa Massimo', *Frankfurter Allgemeine Zeitung*, 1 July 1992 [response to Herta Müller's article of 29 June 1992 in the *Frankfurter Allgemeine Zeitung*].

Rau, Beate, 'Sie kann's nicht ändern. Wir sprachen mit Herta Müller', *Schwäbisches Tagblatt*, 13 December 1992, 22.

Schirrmacher, Frank, 'Bis bald. Seitenblick auf die deutsche Literatur des Herbstes', *Frankfurter Allgemeine Zeitung*, 26 September 1992 [on *Der Fuchs*].

Schlesak, Dieter, 'Wenn die Wörter verhaftet werden. Epochaler Schwanengesang. Eine Bilanz der rumäniendeutschen Literatur', *Die Welt*, 30 May 1992.

Schulte, Bettina, 'Die Macht der Dinge. Die Schriftstellerin Herta Müller las in Freiburg', *Badische Zeitung*, 3 December 1992, 32.

4. Interviews

Auffermann, Verena, 'Gerechtigkeit ist ein Unwort. Ein Gespräch mit der Schriftstellerin Herta Müller über Staatssicherheit, die Sprache und die Macht', *Süddeutsche Zeitung*, 14/15/16 August 1992, 15.

Doerry, Martin and Volker Hage, '"So eisig, kalt und widerlich".
  Die Schriftstellerin Herta Müller über eine Aktion deutscher
  Autoren gegen den Fremdenhaß', *Der Spiegel*, 9 November 1992,
  264–8.
Etzersdorfer, Irene, 'Warum sind Sie enttäuscht, Herta Müller? Ein
  Gespräch mit der rumäniendeutschen Autorin über ihr Land
  nach dem Umsturz', *Die Presse*, 24 October 1992.

1993

1. Primary

*Der Wächter nimmt seinen Kamm. Vom Weggehen und Ausscheren. 94
  Karten in einer Schachtel* (Reinbek bei Hamburg, Rowohlt, 1993).
Niederungen (Reinbek bei Hamburg, Rowohlt, 1993) [first pub-
  lished Kriterion, Bucharest, 1982].
'Staatskinder und Landeskinder. Der innere und der äußere
  Schatten (I)', *Frankfurter Rundschau*, 15 May 1993, 2.
'Staatskinder und Landeskinder. Das Muster der deutschen
  Eigenschaften (II)', *Frankfurter Rundschau*, 22 May 1993.
'Staatskinder und Landeskinder (III)', *Frankfurter Rundschau*, 12
  June 1993 [all of the above three articles reprinted together
  under the title 'Und noch erschrickt unser Herz' in *Hunger und
  Seide*, 19–38].
'ER und SIE. Armut treibt die Menschen an Ceauşescus Grab',
  Frankfurter Allgemeine Zeitung, 23 December 1993 [reprinted in
  Hunger und Seide, 127–35].

2. Secondary: General Literary Studies and Specific Book Reviews

Anon, '*Der Fuchs war damals schon der Jäger*', *World Literature Today*,
  67 (1993), 601-2.
Anon, 'Schön schräg', *Wochenzeitung*, 2 July 1993 [on *Der Wächter*].
Anon, 'Was wird kommen?', *Badische Neueste Nachrichten*, 3 Febru-
  ary 1993 [on *Der Fuchs*].
Broos, Susanne, '*Eine warme Kartoffel ist ein warmes Bett*',
  Börsenblatt, 26 January 1993, 16–19.

Creutziger, Werner, 'Leidendes Land und politischer Weltschmerz', *Neue Deutsche Literatur*, 41 No. 4 (1993), 139–42 [on *Der Fuchs*].

Denneler, Iris, 'Der Fuchs war damals schon der Jäger', Sender Freies Berlin, 5 February 1993 [review on the 'Klassik Plus. Buchzeit' programme].

Hartung, Harald, 'Ausscheren, Einscheren. Herta Müllers apokryphe Postkarten', *Frankfurter Allgemeine Zeitung*, 28 August 1993 [on *Der Wächter*].

Henneberg, Nicole, 'Dann Ruhe', *Basler Zeitung*, 16 July 1993, 37 [on *Der Wächter*].

Hildebrandt, Walter, 'Leiden und Widerhall. Die sarmatische Herausforderung Johannes Bobrowskis und Herta Müllers', *Deutsche Studien*, 30 No. 119 (1993), 195–207.

Jansen, Hans, 'Die Stirnlocke des Diktators', *Westdeutsche Allgemeine Zeitung*, 20 February 1993 [on *Der Fuchs*].

Krauss, Hannes, 'Fremde Blicke. Zur Prosa von Herta Müller und Richard Wagner', in Walter Delabar et al. (eds.), *Neue Generation – neues Erzählen. Deutsche Prosa-Literatur der achtziger Jahre* (Opladen, Westdeutscher Verlag, 1993), 69–76.

Miehe, Renate, 'Warme Kartoffel, warmes Bett. Zugeschnürte Wünsche. Gesammelte Kurzpredigten von Herta Müller', *Frankfurter Allgemeine Zeitung*, 13 January 1993, 28 [on *Eine warme Kartoffel*].

Motzan, Peter, 'Der lange Weg in die Bewährung', *Südostdeutsche Vierteljahresblätter*, 42 No. 2 (1993), 128–34.

Riha, Karl, 'Der Wächter nimmt seinen Kamm', *Frankfurter Rundschau*, 3 July 1993.

Stanzl, Ingeborg Julia Franziska, 'Reisende auf einem Bein' (University of British Columbia MA thesis, 1993).

Stromberg, Kyra, 'Das Mosaik des geheimen Schreckens. Herta Müllers Der Fuchs war damals schon der Jäger', Deutsche Welle, 11 January 1993 [review on the 'Lesezeichen' programme].

Utz, Peter, 'Kartengrüsse aus Nirgendwo. Herta Müllers Collagen vom "Weggehen" und "Ausscheren"', *Tages Anzeiger*, 3 July 1993 [on *Der Wächter*].

3. Secondary: Miscellaneous

Anon, 'Eine Sprache, die unter die Haut geht. Herta Müller las im Literaturarchiv', *Marbacher Zeitung*, 19 March 1993, 16.

Anon, 'Nur ein Schwall poetischer Vernebelung. Herta Müller las
   vor großem Publikum im Deutschen Literaturarchiv',
   Ludwigsburger Kreiszeitung, 20 March 1993, 12.
Cosack, Bettina, 'Noch erschrickt das Herz. Herta Müller über
   deutsche Weltoffenheit', *Berliner Zeitung*, 19 April 1993, 23.
Ferchl, Irene, 'Bilder statt Geschichten. Herta Müller liest im
   Marbacher Literaturarchiv', *Stuttgarter Zeitung*, 19 March 1993,
   25.
Jessen, Jens, 'Der gewendete Handschuh. Reportage. "Nicht fremd
   und nicht zu Haus" (ZDF)', *Frankfurter Allgemeine Zeitung*, 9
   February 1993, 28 [preview of film looking at foreign writers in
   Germany, including Herta Müller].
Scheer, Udo, 'Von der Verweigerung, Deutsche zu sein. Die
   rümaniendeutsche Schriftstellerin Herta Müller las in Jena',
   Neue Zeit, 5 October 1993, 14.
Widmann, Arno, 'Essen mit Herta Müller', *Vogue (Deutsch)*, No.1,
   January 1993, 112–13.

4. Interviews

Anon, '"Ich glaube, alle Diktatoren ähneln sich". Ein Gespräch mit
   der Schriftstellerin Herta Müller über Literatur, Politik und
   Sprache', *Straubinger Tagblatt*, 22 January 1993.
Furtado, Maria Teresa Dias, 'Interview mit Herta Müller', *Runa*
   (1993), No.1, 189–95.

1994

1. Primary

Herztier. Roman (Reinbek bei Hamburg, Rowohlt, 1994).
Der Fuchs war damals schon der Jäger. Roman (Reinbek bei Hamburg,
   Rowohlt, 1994) [first published Reinbek bei Hamburg, Rowohlt,
   1992].
'Die Nacht sie hat Pantoffeln an. Über Inge Müllers Gedichte',
   Literaturmagazin (1994), No. 34, 14–18.
'Das Ticken der Norm', *Die Zeit*, 14 January 1994, 49–50 [reprinted
   in Edwin Kratschmer (ed.), *Dem Erinnern eine Chance. Jenaer
   Poetik-Vorlesungen 'Zu Beförderung der Humanität' 1993/94*

(Cologne, Heinrich-Böll-Stiftung, 1995), 107–15, and in *Hunger und Seide*, 88–100].

'Am Ende war es keiner gewesen. Vor zwanzig Jahren starb die Schriftstellerin Marieluise Fleißer', *die tageszeitung*, 2 February 1994, 13.

'Von Menschen nicht mehr zu bewohnen. Die serbische Landkarte ersetzt das Gewissen. Über die Wurzeln nationaler Propaganda', *Frankfurter Allgemeine Zeitung*, 27 April 1994, 37 [reprinted with the title 'Auf die Gedanken fällt Erde' in *Hunger und Seide*, 164–71].

'Zehn Finger werden keine Utopie', Südwestfunk, 17 July 1994 [radio essay on the 'Blick in die Zeit' programme].

'Meine Jahre mit Helmut Kohl', *Die Zeit*, 2 September 1994, 56.

'Man spürte sie lauern', *Stuttgarter Zeitung*, 29 October 1994, 50 [extract from *Herztier*].

'Von der gebrechlichen Einrichtung der Welt. Rede anläßlich der Entgegennahme des Kleist-Preises', *Neue Zürcher Zeitung*, 1 November 1994, 24; also in *Kleist-Jahrbuch*, 16 (1995), 14–19 [reprinted in *Hunger und Seide*, 7–15].

2. Secondary: General Literary Studies and Specific Book Reviews

Apel, Friedmar, 'Kirschkern Wahrheit. Inmitten beschädigter Paradiese. Herta Müllers *Herztier*', *Frankfurter Allgemeine Zeitung*, 4 October 1994, 16.

Bartens, Gisela, 'Wie das Singen von tiefem Gras', *Kleine Zeitung*, 3 December 1994 [on *Herztier*].

Dattenberger, Simone, 'Dichtes Netz aus Stimmungen gewoben. Leben in einem Terrorsystem. Herta Müllers Roman *Herztier* ist bei Rowohlt erschienen', *Münchner Merkur*, 22 November 1994.

Falcke, Eberhard, 'Mit unveränderter poetischer Intensität durchqueil Heila Müller im Roman *Herztier* das ihr geläufige Unglücksgelände', *Süddeutsche Zeitung*, 5/6 November 1994.

Kolbe, Uwe, 'Kosmos der Angst', *Die Woche*, 14 October 1994, 46 [on *Herztier*].

Kraft, Thomas, 'Erinnerungsbewältigung. Herta Müllers Roman *Herztier*', *Freitag*, 7 October 1994.

Kraft, Thomas, 'Das Herztier in die Knie zwingen. Der Kontrolle entgeht man nicht – Herta Müllers jüngster Roman', *Stuttgarter Zeitung*, 21 October 1994, 22 [on *Herztier*].

Kroner, Michael, 'Herztier', *Südostdeutsche Vierteljahresblätter*, 43 No. 4 (1994), 349–50.

Lenhardt, Dieter, 'Die Sprache der Quitten', *Die Presse*, 1 October 1994 [on *Herztier*].

Liessmann, Konrad Paul, 'Die liebsten Personen sind zerbrochen und tot', *Der Standard*, 30 August 1994 [on *Herztier*].

Lorenz, Christian, 'Nieren und Zungen im Kühlschrank. Über ängstliche Seelen in der Diktatur. Die rumäniendeutsche Autorin Herta Müller legt ihren Roman *Herztier* vor', *Deutsches Allgemeines Sonntagsblatt*, 21 October 1994, 24.

Luchsinger, Martin, 'Der Roman der Diktatur. Herta Müllers *Herztier*. Leben und Sterben in Rumänien', *Tages Anzeiger*, 19 December 1994.

Mahlberg, Gerhard, 'Herztier', *Neue Literatur* (1994), No. 4, 103–8.

Mahlberg, Gerhard, 'Herztier', Deutschland Radio, 16 October 1994 [review on the 'Büchermarkt' programme].

Matt, Beatrice von, 'Im Körper das mitgebrachte Land. Herta Müllers Roman *Herztier*', *Neue Zürcher Zeitung*, 29 September 1994.

Michaelis, Rolf, 'In der Angst zu Haus. Ein Überlebensbuch. Herta Müllers Roman *Herztier*', *Die Zeit*, 7 October 1994, 8.

Mischke, Roland, 'Soziale Realität in surrealen Szenen. Herta Müllers neues Werk – ein Buch gegen das Vergessen', *Mitteldeutsche Zeitung*, 14 September 1994 [on *Herztier*].

Moritz, Rainer, 'Spiegeleier auf dem Bügeleisen', *Rheinischer Merkur*, 7 October 1994 [on *Herztier*].

Ottmers, Clemens, 'Schreiben und Leben. Herta Müller, *Der Teufel sitzt im Spiegel. Wie Wahrnehmung sich erfindet (1991)*', in Paul Michael Lützeler (ed.), *Poetik der Autoren. Beiträge zur deutschsprachigen Gegenwartsliteratur* (Frankfurt am Main, Fischer, 1994), 279–94.

Preisendörfer, Bruno, 'Wem der Tod pfeift. Eine Prosa, die den Geschmack der Angst hervorruft. Herta Müllers *Herztier* auf dem Sprung von Rumänien nach Deutschland', *Der Tagesspiegel*, 2/3 October 1994, 5.

Ramm, Klaus, 'Herztier', Sender Freies Berlin, 10 November 1994 [review on the 'Buchzeit' programme].

Richard, Christine, 'Wunderbar nüchterne Selbsterdichtung', *Basler Zeitung*, 5 October 1994 [on *Herztier*].

Roggemann, Lutz, 'Herztier', *Deutsche Bücher*, 24 No. 3 (1994), 204–6.

Röhr, Esther, 'Der Tod der Toten. Herta Müllers Roman *Herztier*', *Frankfurter Rundschau*, 5 October 1994.

Schandor, Werner, 'Holzmelonen und Blechschafe. Zeugnis einer bedrückenden Enge. Herta Müllers Roman *Herztier*', *Wiener Zeitung*, 11 November 1994.

Schulte, Bettina, 'Menschen, die in der Angst zu Hause sind', *Badische Zeitung*, 12 November 1994, 6 [on *Herztier*].

Senz, Ingomar, *Die Donauschwaben* (München, Langen Müller, 1994) [refers to the *Aktiongruppe Banat*, including Herta Müller].

Törne, Dorothea von, 'Todesnetze, verbotene Früchte. Herta Müller entwirft in *Herztier* ein surreales Panorama der Diktatur', *Wochenpost*, 11 August 1994, 23.

Zintz, Karin, 'Anwachsen gegen den Tod. Tragik des Widerstands. Herta Müllers neuer Roman *Herztier*', *Eßlinger Zeitung*, 1 October 1994.

3. Secondary: Miscellaneous

Anon, '"Unschuldige Sprache?" Günter Grass und Herta Müller im Streit', *Basler Zeitung*, 21 May 1994.

Anon, 'PEN-Kongreß. Streit zwischen Grass und Müller', *Die Welt*, 21 May 1994.

Anon, 'Kleist-Preis für Pinzetten-Prosa. Herta Müller ausgezeichnet', *Arbeiter Zeitung*, 21 October 1994.

Anon, 'Mit dem Herztier. Kleist-Preis für Herta Müller', *Stuttgarter Zeitung*, 21 October 1994, 23.

Anon, 'Selbstprovinzialisierung', *Süddeutsche Zeitung*, 21 October 1994, 13 [on Herta Müller winning the Kleist Prize].

Anon, 'Kleist-Preisträgerin Herta Müller warnt vor Gewalt und Radikalismus', *Frankfurter Rundschau*, 22 October 1994.

Baron, Ulrich, 'Literatur im Zeichen des Kranichs', *Rheinischer Merkur*, 4 October 1994.

Grack, Günter, 'Was der Kleist-Preis wert ist', *Freitag*, 21 October 1994, 19.

Gutschke, Irmtraud, 'Ewiges Trauma', *Neues Deutschland*, 22/23 October 1994, 2.

Laudenbach, Peter, 'Prosa, die schockiert. Herta Müller wird mit dem Kleist-Preis geehrt', *Berliner Zeitung*, 21 October 1994, 26.

Ostmann, Sabine, 'Angst wird zum Zuhause. Herta Müller las in Saarbrücken aus ihrem neuen Roman', *Saarbrücker Zeitung*, 19 October 1994, 12.

Scheer, Udo, 'Das Ticken der Norm. Herta Müller hielt in Jena eine Vorlesung in der Reihe "Literatur zur Beförderung der Humanität"', *Neue Zeit*, 7 May 1994, 14.

Schreiber, Ulrich, 'Von der Schuld der Sprache in einer gewalttätigen Welt. Podiumsdiskussion mit Grass, Müller u.a. auf der Tagung des westdeutschen PEN-Zentrums', *Frankfurter Rundschau*, 21 May 1994, 9.

Zintz, Karin, 'Zwischen Emotion und Distanz. Schriftstellerin Herta Müller erhält den Kleistpreis 1994', *Münchner Merkur*, 21 October 1994.

1995

1. Primary

Hunger und Seide. Essays (Reinbek bei Hamburg, Rowohlt, 1995).

Der Mensch ist ein großer Fasan auf der Welt. Roman (Reinbek bei Hamburg, Rowohlt, 1995) [first published Berlin, Rotbuch, 1986].

Reisende auf einem Bein (Reinbek bei Hamburg, Rowohlt, 1995) [first published Berlin, Rotbuch, 1989].

'"Sag, daß du fünfzehn bist". *weiter leben*. Ruth Klüger', *Runa* 23 (1995), 385–400.

'Auszug aus *Der Teufel sitzt im Spiegel*', *Orte*, 20 No. 93 (1995), 46.

'Wahrheit danach. Warum wir aus Diktaturen nichts lernen', *Frankfurter Allgemeine Zeitung*, 4 May 1995.

'Wenn mein Körper mich im Stich läßt. "Ich werde mein Land nicht als Staatsgast besuchen, was stellen die sich vor? Aber die Sprache rächt sich an mir, je älter ich werde, umso öfter träume ich auf rumänisch. Und ich kann mich nicht dagegen wehren". Zum Tod des bis zuletzt auf der Pariser "Cité" staatenlos lebenden Schriftstellers E. M. Cioran', *die tageszeitung*, 23 June 1995, 17.

'Es möge deine letzte Trauer sein. Notizen und Gedichte des iranischen Exilautors Said', *Die Zeit*, 11 August 1995, 40.

'Der Himmelsschlüssel. Rede bei der Übergabe des Stadtschreiberpreises von Bergen-Enkheim und des dazugehörigen Schlüssels am Vorabend des Berger Marktes', *Frankfurter Rundschau*, 4 September 1995, 17.

2. Secondary: General Literary Studies and Specific Book Reviews

Anon, 'Eine Autorin, die sprachmächtig Macht attackiert', *Salzburger Nachrichten*, 20 May 1995 [on *Hunger*].

Anon, 'Keine vermessenen Glücksgedanken. Poetischer Scharfsinn, politische Integrität in Herta Müllers Essays', *Tiroler Tageszeitung*, 4 October 1995 [on *Hunger*].

Achermann, Erika, 'Der Plan der eigenen Vernunft', *Tages Anzeiger*, 15 June 1995 [portrait].

Achermann, Erika, 'Schule des Widerstands. Herta Müllers Essays', *Die Presse. Bücher Pick*, No. 3, August 1995, 23 [on *Hunger*].

Cramer, Sibylle, 'Richtige Worte, falsche Taufen. Traktate einer Moralistin. Herta Müllers publizistische Gelegenheitsarbeiten, als Essays präsentiert', *Süddeutsche Zeitung*, 10/11 June 1995.

Engler, Jürgen, 'Erfahrung, leibhaft', *Neue Deutsche Literatur*, 43 No. 1 (1995), 174–6.

Fitzel, Thomas, 'Die Sprache, ein Garten aus Ängsten. Alltäglich erfahrbare Abstumpfung und Entmündigung. Herta Müllers biographischer Roman *Herztier*', *die tageszeitung*, 25 April 1995, 16.

Gauß, Karl-Markus, 'Ein volles Leben im leeren. Herta Müllers Reden und Einsprüche aus den letzten Jahren', *Frankfurter Allgemeine Zeitung*, 11 April 1995.

Hinck, Walter, 'Das mitgebrachte Land. Zur Verleihung des Kleist-Preises 1994 an Herta Müller', *Sinn und Form*, 47 No. 1 (1995), 141–6; also in *Kleist-Jahrbuch*, 16 (1995), 6–13.

Jenny-Ebeling, Charitas, 'Herta Müller. Ein Gesicht und ein Thema', *Neue Zürcher Zeitung*, 18 July 1995, 35.

Kegelmann, René, *An den Grenzen des Nichts, dieser Sprache. Zur Situation rumäniendeutscher Literatur der achtziger Jahre in der Bundesrepublik Deutschland* (Bielefeld, Aisthesis, 1995) [explores Herta Müller's work amongst others].

Koopmann, Helmut, 'Rede zur Verleihung des Kleist-Preis 1994 an Herta Müller', *Kleist-Jahrbuch*, 16 (1995), 3–5.

Kopplin, Wolfgang, '*Herztier*', *Bayern Kurier*, 3 June 1995, 16.

Kraft, Thomas, 'Mißtrauisch und hellhörig', *Freitag*, 7 April 1995 [on *Hunger*].

Kratschmer, Edwin, 'Herta Müller. Von der Vernormung des Menschen', in Kratschmer (ed.), *Dem Erinnern eine Chance* (1994), 116.

Krumbholz, Martin, 'Hunger und Seide', *Die Woche*, 24 March 1995.

Kuhnle, Till R., 'La résistance des monades. *Herztier* de Herta Müller', *Germanica*, 17 (1995), 25–38.

Lauer, Ilse, 'Freundschaft in Zeiten der Diktatur', *Südostdeutsche Vierteljahresblätter*, 44 (1995), 143–7 [on *Herztier*].

Luchsinger, Martin, 'Aufblitzende Dramatik', *Tages Anzeiger*, 18 May 1995 [on *Hunger*].

Mischke, Roland, 'Hunger und Seide', *General-Anzeiger*, 3/4 June 1995, 11.

Mitgutsch, Anna, 'Widerstand als moralische Geste', *Der Standard*, 7 April 1995 [on *Hunger*].

Overath, Angelika, 'Unter dem Ticken der Norm', *Neue Zürcher Zeitung*, 11 May 1995, 33 [on *Hunger*].

Schlaffer, Hannelore, 'Liegt Deutschland in Rumänien? Herta Müllers gesammelte Berichte und Reden über das beschädigte Leben in den Diktaturen', *Frankfurter Rundschau*, 21 March 1995, 25 [on *Hunger*].

Schuh, Franz, 'Die Tradition der Machtfeindschaft. Herta Müllers Essays *Hunger und Seide* haben ihre Sache auf die Angst gebaut', *Die Zeit*, 7 April 1995, 8.

Starkmann, Alfred, 'Wenn die Ratio durchgeht. Fortwährend betroffen. Herta Müller rechnet weiter ab', *Die Welt*, 8 July 1995 [on *Hunger* and *Der Mensch*].

Törne, Dorothea von, 'Zwischen den Sprachböden. Herta Müllers poetische Stellungnahmen zu Fragen der Zeit', *Der Tagesspiegel*, 5 June 1995 [on *Hunger*].

Willems, Gottfried, 'Herta Müller', in Kratschmer (ed.), *Dem Erinnern eine Chance* (1994), 115–16.

Zierden, Josef, 'Herta Müller', in Heinz Ludwig Arnold (ed.), *Kritisches Lexikon zur deutschsprachigen Gegenwartsliteratur* (Munich, Text und Kritik, 1978 ff.), 50 Nlg. (1995), 1–8 + bibliography A–G.

3. Secondary: Miscellaneous

Anon, 'Herta Müller gegen Vereinigung der deutschen PEN-Clubs', *Die Welt*, 6 January 1995.

Anon, 'Herta Müller droht mit Austritt aus vereintem PEN-Club', *Der Tagesspiegel*, 6 January 1995, 20.

Anon, 'Berichte vom Überlebenskampf. Herta Müller wird neue Stadtschreiberin in Bergen-Enkheim', *Frankfurter Rundschau*, 9 June 1995.

Anon, '"Alles, was wir wissen, ist Gegenwart". Bonn bietet Literatur pur. Im Mittelpunkt. Poetik-Vorlesungen mit Herta Müller', *General-Anzeiger*, 14 June 1995, 14.

Anon, 'Neue Proteste gegen Friedenspreis des deutschen Buchhandels für Annemarie Schimmel. Autoren raten dem Bundespräsidenten Herzog von der Verleihung ab. Kritik an Orientalistin bekräftigt', *Stuttgarter Zeitung*, 6 September 1995, 25 [Herta Müller signs open letter from, amongst others, Ingrid Bacher, Erich Loest and Günter Grass].

Anon, 'Europäischer Preis für Herta Müller', *Stuttgarter Zeitung*, 12 December 1995 [Herta Müller awarded the European *Prix Aristeion*].

Geißler, Cornelia, 'Loest in Haft – der PEN schwieg. Die Schriftstellerin Herta Müller lehnt die Vereinigung der deutschen PEN-Zentren ab', *Berliner Zeitung*, 8 March 1995, 37.

Grohmer, Ulrich, 'Ein Ufer finden für ein Leben in Freiheit. Zu Gast in der literaturWERKstatt Pankow. Herta Müller und Richard Wagner', *Neues Deutschland*, 24 April 1995, 10.

Gutschke, Irmtraud, 'Die Mauer wieder aufbauen? Herta Müller protestiert gegen gesamtdeutschen PEN', *Neues Deutschland*, 6 January 1995.

Jessen, Jens, 'Zweierlei Friede. Deutsche Szene. Die Schimmelgegner in Berlin', *Frankfurter Allgemeine Zeitung*, 5 October 1995, 43.

Löffler, Sigrid, 'Gibt es den Euro-Roman? Eine EU-Jury hat ihn gefunden. Unsere Autorin hat heftig mitgesucht', *Weltwoche*, 14 December 1995 [Herta Müller awarded the European *Prix Aristeion*].

Losch, Roland, 'Alte "Halunken". Autoren gegen PEN-Vereinigung', *Münchner Merkur*, 19 January 1995 [Herta Müller's objections to the merger are quoted].

Lumme, Christoph, 'Die Wanderin zwischen den Welten. Herta
Müller an der Ruhr-Uni', *Ruhr Nachrichten*, 5 December 1995.
Serke, Jürgen, '"Da nehme ich meinen Hut". Viele Schriftsteller
protestieren heftig gegen die kommende PEN-Vereinigung',
Weltwoche, 12 January 1995 [Herta Müller's objections are again
quoted].
Steinbicker, Ute, 'Merkwürdig egozentrisch', *Frankfurter Rundschau*,
6 April 1995 [reader's letter responding to Hannelore Schlaffer's
review of *Hunger und Seide*].

4. Interviews

Broos, Susanne, 'Lebenslärm zum Schreiben. Ein Gespräch mit der
neuen Stadtschreiberin von Bergen-Enkheim Herta Müller über
ihre Pläne für nächstes Jahr', *Frankfurter Rundschau*, 1 September
1995, 21.
Dobler, Alexander, 'Der Wind spricht nicht, sondern die Menschen
sprechen. Die Erzählerin Herta Müller über menschliches
Verhalten, die Macht und die Sprache', *Frankfurter Rundschau*,
12 July 1995, 7.
Kroeger-Groth, Elisabeth, '"Der Brunnen ist kein Fenster und kein
Spiegel, oder Wie Wahrnehmung sich erfindet". Ein Gespräch
mit Herta Müller', *Diskussion Deutsch*, 26 (1995), 223–30.

1996

1. Primary

In der Falle (Göttingen, Wallstein, 1996) [Bonner Poetik-Vorlesung
Band II].
Herztier. Roman (Reinbek bei Hamburg, Rowohlt, 1996) [first pub-
lished Reinbek bei Hamburg, Rowohlt, 1994].
Drückender Tango. Erzählungen (Reinbek bei Hamburg, Rowohlt,
1996) [selection of *Erzählungen* previously published in
Niederungen and *Barfüßiger Februar*].
The Land of Green Plums, translated by Michael Hofmann (New
York, Metropolitan Books, 1996) [English translation of *Herztier*].
Hartedier, translated by Ria van Hengel (Amsterdam, De Geus,
1996) [Dutch translation of *Herztier*].

La piel del zorro, translated by Juan José del Solar (Barcelona, Plaza and Janes, 1996) [Spanish translation of *Der Fuchs war damals schon der Jäger*].

'Das kleingewürfelte Glück. Erinnerung an den Dichter Rolf Bossert', *Frankfurter Allgemeine Zeitung*, 17 February 1996, 27.

'Das Haar auf der Schulter. Fünf Texte zur Messe in C-Dur von Franz Schubert', *Frankfurter Rundschau*, 26/27 May 1996.

'Zungenspäße und Büßerschnee. Wie Helmut Böttiger mich durch "Orte Paul Celans" führte', *Die Zeit*, 6 December 1996, 3.

2. Secondary: General Literary Studies and Specific Book Reviews

Anon, 'The Land of Green Plums', *Kirkus Reviews*, 15 September 1996, 1347 [on *Herztier*].

Anon, 'The Land of Green Plums', *Publishers' Weekly*, 7 October 1996, 60–1.

Anon, 'The Land of Green Plums', *Library Journal*, 1 November 1996, 108.

Anon, 'The Land of Green Plums', *Booklist*, 15 November 1996, 570.

Bauer, Karin, 'Tabus der Wahrnehmung. Reflexion und Geschichte in Herta Müllers Prosa', *German Studies Review*, 14 No. 2 (1996), 257–78.

Bauer, Karin, 'Zur Objektwerdung der Frau in Herta Müllers *Der Mensch ist ein großer Fasan auf der Welt*', *seminar*, 32 No. 2 (1996), 143-54.

Haupt-Cucuiu, Herta, *Eine Poesie der Sinne. Herta Müllers Diskurs des Alleinseins und seine Wurzeln* (Paderborn, Igel, 1996).

Kegelmann, René, 'Hunger und Seide', *Südostdeutsche Vierteljahresblätter*, 45 (1996), 146–7.

Vogelaar, Jacq, 'Angst oogsten', *De Groene Amsterdammer*, 30 October 1996, 42 [on *Herztier*].

Wolff, Larry, 'Strangers in a strange land: Herta Müller's novel centres on the German minority in Romania', *The New York Times Book Review*, 1 December 1996, 36 [on *Herztier*].

3. Secondary: Miscellaneous

Anon, 'Nach Slowenien. Handke liest, Herta Müller übt Kritik', *Frankfurter Allgemeine Zeitung*, 9 February 1996, 36 [Müller's criticisms of EU attitude to Serbian leaders are quoted].

Bissinger, Manfred, 'Keine Zeile, kein Wort', *Die Woche*, 2 August 1996 [concerns Herta Müller's resignation from the PEN-Club].

Broos, Susanne, 'Wo der Konjunktiv regiert. Herta Müller las im Presseclub aus *Hunger und Seide*', *Frankfurter Rundschau*, 9 February 1996, 24.

Broos, Susanne, 'Die Kehle geschnürt, der Puls gehetzt. Herta Müller, Stadtschreiberin von Bergen-Enkheim, gab eine Abschiedslesung', *Frankfurter Rundschau*, 12 August 1996, 16.

1997

1. Primary

Heute wär ich mir lieber nicht begegnet. Roman (Reinbek bei Hamburg, Rowohlt, 1997).

Hunger und Seide. Essays (Reinbek bei Hamburg, Rowohlt, 1997) [first published Reinbek bei Hamburg, Rowohlt, 1995].

'Die Klette am Knie', *Akzente*, 44 No. 2 (1997), 104-12.

Le renard était déjà le chasseur, translated by Claire de Oliveira (Paris, Seuil, 1997) [French translation of *Der Fuchs war damals schon der Jäger*].

'The red flower and the rod', *Women in German Yearbook*, 13 (1997), 1-6.

'Sarkuhi ist unschuldig. Wie halten wir es mit der Freiheit des Geistes? Ein Appell', *Die Zeit*, 1 August 1997.

'Heute wär ich mir lieber nicht begegnet', *Neue Zürcher Zeitung*, 19 August 1997 [a pre-publication extract from the novel].

2. Secondary: General Literary Studies and Specific Book Reviews

Apel, Friedmar, 'Turbatverse. Ästhetik, Mystik und Politik bei Herta Müller', *Akzente*, 44 No. 2 (1997), 113–25.

Beste, Gisela, 'Kommunikation und Identität in Herta Müllers Erzählung *Der Mensch ist ein großer Fasan auf der Welt*', *Deutschunterricht* (Berlin), 50 No. 9 (1997), 124–9.

Eke, Norbert Otto, '"Sein Leben machen / ist nicht, / sein Glück machen / mein Herr." Zum Verhältnis von Ästhetik und Politik in Herta Müllers Nachrichten aus Rumänien', *Jahrbuch der Deutschen Schillergesellschaft*, 41 (1997), 481-509.

Glajar, Valentina, 'Banat-Swabian, Romanian, and German: conflicting identities in Herta Müller's *Herztier*', *Monatshefte*, 89 No. 4 (1997), 521–40.

Hager, Martin, 'Literaturschauplatz Siebenbürgen. Transsylvanischer Mythos des 19. und spießig-totalitäre Realität des 20. Jahrhunderts', *die tageszeitung*, 4/5 October 1997 [on *Heute* and *Niederungen*].

Harnisch, Antje, '"Ausländerin im Ausland". Herta Müllers *Reisende auf einem Bein*, *Monatshefte*, 89 No. 4 (1997), 507–20.

Kebir, Sabine, 'So rot wie ein Beet Klatschmohn. Immer wieder Rumänien. Herta Müllers fortgesetzte Rückschau auf die Zeit der Diktatur', *die tageszeitung*, 15 October 1997, 9 [on *Heute*].

Köhnen, Ralph (ed.), *Der Druck der Erfahrung treibt die Sprache in die Dichtung. Bildlichkeit in Texten Herta Müllers* (Frankfurt, Peter Lang, 1997).

Kraft, Thomas, 'Refugium und Protest. Herta Müllers Poetikvorlesungen', *Freitag*, 7 March 1997, 12 [on *In der Falle*].

Krauss, Hannes, 'Innenansichten', *Freitag*, 10 October 1997 [on *Heute*].

Krumbholz, Martin, 'Vom Umgang mit der Angst', *Süddeutsche Zeitung*, 30 January 1997 [on *In der Falle*].

Melzer, Gerhard, 'Verkrallt in Aussichtslosigkeit. Eine rumänische Kindheit. Zu Herta Müller und ihrem Roman *Herztier*', in Wernfried Hofmeister und Bernd Steinbauer (eds.) *Durch aubenteuer muess man wagen vil. Festschrift für Anton Schwob zum 60. Geburtstag* (Innsbruck, Institut für Germanistik, 1997), 291–7.

Meudal, Gérard, 'Engrenage infernal. Pointilliste Herta Müller dépeint la vie quotidienne sous Ceauşescu jusqu'au cauchemar', *Le Monde des Livres*, 3 May 1997, 5 [on *Der Fuchs*].

Moritz, Rainer, 'Tod so rot wie Klatschmohn', *Rheinischer Merkur*, 17 October 1997 [on *Heute*].

Ohland, Angelika, '"Ich bin bestellt". Herta Müllers neuer Roman kreist um einen einzigen Satz und um das Leben unter der Diktatur', *Deutsches Allgemeines Sonntagsblatt*, 17 October 1997 [on *Heute*].

Osterkamp, Ernst, 'Das verkehrte Glück. Herta Müllers Roman aus der Diktatur', *Frankfurter Allgemeine Zeitung*, 14 October 1997 [on *Heute*].

Scheer, Udo, 'Herta Müller begegnet einer bestellten Frau', *Die Welt*, 14 October 1997 [on *Heute*].

Steets, Angelika, 'Herta Müller. Sprache und Identität. *Der Mensch ist ein großer Fasan auf der Welt'*, Deutschunterricht (Berlin), 50 No. 9 (1997), 130–8.

3. Secondary: Miscellaneous

Anon, 'Das tägliche Leben. Herta Müller liest in Niedlichs Salon', *Stuttgarter Zeitung*, 30 April 1997.
Anon, 'Der deutsche Literatur-Kanon. Was sollen Schüler lesen?', *Die Zeit*, 16 May 1997 [Herta Müller's views are canvassed amongst others].
Anon, 'In der Gesellschaft der Spitzel. Autorin Herta Müller war Gast auf Schloß Mauterndorf', *Salzburger Nachrichten*, 14 June 1997.
Anon, 'Morgen zu Herta Müller ins Literaturhaus', *Frankfurter Rundschau*, 22 September 1997.
Anon, 'Literaturpreis der Stadt Graz geht an Herta Müller', *Tages Anzeiger*, 8 November 1997.
Harms, Ingeborg, 'Die Toga um den warmen Leib geschlungen. Aus den deutschen Zeitschriften. Wie sich die Kunst des zwanzigsten Jahrhunderts dem Totalitarismus stellt', *Frankfurter Allgemeine Zeitung*, 31 May 1997 [refers to Friedmar Apel's article on Herta Müller in *Akzente*].
Tolksdorf, Stefan, 'Ein Rathaus für die Welt der Bücher. Das Freiburger Literaturgespräch bietet viel Qualität und wenig Geschwätz', *Stuttgarter Zeitung*, 13 November 1997, 27 [Herta Müller amongst others is quoted].

4. Interviews

'Vor Renegaten sollten wir uns verneigen. Gespräch mit Gernot Facius und Adelbert Reif', *Die Welt*, 1 December 1997, 9.
Müller, Wolfgang, '"Poesie ist ja nichts Angenehmes". Gespräch mit Herta Müller', *Monatshefte*, 89 No. 4 (1997), 468–76.

1998

1. Primary

The Land of Green Plums, translated by Michael Hofmann (London, Granta, 1998) [English translation of *Herztier*, first published New York, Metropolitán Books, 1996].

'Die Geschichte vom Huhn. Rede zur Verleihung des Franz-Nabl-Literaturpreises', *Neue Zürcher Zeitung*, 21 March 1998, 52.

2. Secondary: General Literary Studies and Specific Book Reviews

Melzer, Gerhard, 'Die abgeschnittenen Finger. Herta Müller und ihr doppelt belichtetes Rumänien', *Neue Zürcher Zeitung*, 21/22 March 1998.

Overath, Angelika, 'Die Bestellte. Herta Müllers neuer Roman', *Neue Zürcher Zeitung*, 21/22 March 1998 [on *Heute*].

Steiner, George, 'You're ruled by hooligans. Your friends spy on you. Hellish, isn't it?', *The Observer*, 30 August 1998 [on the English translation of *Herztier*].

Thomson, Ian, 'Government by ghouls', *The Guardian*, 25 July 1998 [on the English translation of *Herztier*].

3. Secondary: Miscellaneous

Scheer, Udo, 'Nacktes, klopfendes Herztier. Leiden an der Diktatur: Herta Müller erhält den Impac-Literaturpreis', *Die Welt*, 20 May 1998.

4. Interviews

'Die ungewohnte Gewöhnlichkeit bei Oskar Pastior', *wespennest*, 110 (1998), 80-6.

'"Wie in einem Schlund" – Wo liegt Rumänien? Gespräch mit Sascha Bunge und Titus Faschina', *tageszeitung*, 14 March 1998, 13–14.

Staunton, Denis, 'The spy who loved me', *The Guardian*, 7 July 1998.

Index